Genghis Khan

A Captivating Guide to the Founder of the Mongol Empire and His Conquests Which Resulted in the Largest Contiguous Empire in History

Free Bonus from Captivating History (Available for a Limited time)

Hi History Lovers!

Now you have a chance to join our exclusive history list so you can get your first history ebook for free as well as discounts and a potential to get more history books for free! Simply visit the link below to join.

Captivatinghistory.com/ebook

Also, make sure to follow us on Facebook, Twitter and Youtube by searching for Captivating History.

Contents

INTRODUCTION 1

CHAPTER 1 – THE MONGOLIAN STEPPE.................................4

CHAPTER 2 – TEMÜJIN...10

CHAPTER 3 – BECOMING GENGHIS KHAN 16

CHAPTER 4 – BUILDING THE MONGOL EMPIRE 24

CHAPTER 5 – LIFE IN GENGHIS KHAN'S EMPIRE 34

CHAPTER 6 – MILITARY GENIUS 41

CHAPTER 7 – INNOVATION..51

CHAPTER 8 - DEATH AND SUCCESSION..............................58

CHAPTER 9 – THE MONGOL EMPIRE AFTER GENGHIS KHAN 65

CHAPTER 10 – PAX MONGOLICA 74

CHAPTER 11 – THE END OF AN EMPIRE 82

CONCLUSION 89

REFERENCES..93

Introduction

Around the year 1162, near the modern capital of Mongolia, a baby boy was born into a fractious and violent world. The birth of this child must have caused quite a stir among the members of the nomadic tribe that he had been born into; word soon traveled that the son of Yesükhei, the Borjigin tribal leader, had been born clutching a blood clot in his tiny hand. Mongol folklore hailed this as a sign that the child would grow up to be a great leader of men, but perhaps history would interpret the baby's gruesome prize as a foreshadowing of the bloodshed that would accompany his life and his legacy.

The child was given the name Temüjin, meaning blacksmith. While it may seem like a name that implies the child should grow up to work with iron, it was actually chosen by his father Yesükhei after capturing a man named Temüjin-üge from a rival tribal group—one of the Tatars. It was an ironic twist for young Temüjin. Little did Yesükhei know that this rivalry with the Tatars would prove to be both his own undoing and the catalyst that propelled his son forward in his journey to becoming the leader of the largest contiguous empire the world would ever see.

Tribal history and family legends were incredibly important to the Mongol tribes. As nomads, they had very little built heritage or material possessions to wield as symbols of their power. The mythology and folklore that built up around a tribe was a huge part of what made them powerful, as the stories we are told shape who we become. As the son of a tribal leader, the auspicious birth of Temüjin became all the more meaningful as the tribe recounted the bardic tales of their origins. The family of Yesükhei had always been considered to have divine origins. His earliest ancestor was believed to be a grey wolf, endowed with divine power that passed down to his ancestors. *The Secret History of the Mongols*, the ancient text that describes Mongol history and the life of Temüjin, states, "There was once a blue-gray wolf who was born with his destiny preordained by Heaven Above. His wife was a fallow doe."

Every Mongol child born into the tribe would have been made very aware of the long line of tribesmen he had come from since ancestral worship was an important aspect of Mongol culture at this time. Temüjin would have grown up knowing that his family history was prestigious, and he probably knew about the magical sign at his birth that was supposed to predestine him to greatness. As he grew up, he would learn how to take advantage of the power of reputation. He would master the art of ensuring that both his friends and his enemies only knew what he wanted them to know so that he could control how they perceived him and exploit their weaknesses. He would also use the fear he commanded to control the outcome of wars without the need to ever fight a battle. Yet when warfare was required, he never shied away from it.

The name Temüjin means little to most people, but the name Genghis Khan is still a potent one. He is one of the most recognized characters from history, both respected and reviled, depending on one's perspective. The word "character" is a good choice here because the picture we have built up in our collective imaginations of Genghis Khan, fed by movies and stories, is of a character rather than a real man. And yet, much of the mythology surrounding him is true; many of those amazing quotable facts we hear about Genghis

Khan are based in truth. For example, it is true that a surprisingly large proportion of the world's population is indeed descended from Genghis Khan; as many as 0.5% of the male population carries his DNA. Another often quoted fact is that the Mongol conquests resulted in a higher percentage of deaths than the World Wars; again, this is true. However, there are contradictions that come as a surprise. He was incredibly tolerant of other cultures, promoting religious freedom and diversity. He also treated his people well, as long as they obeyed his laws. It appears that he believed in meritocracy, equality, and fairness. So, how do we square the bloodthirsty genocidal villain with the progressive, religiously tolerant leader?

In many ways, the story of Temüjin, and Genghis Khan as he would later be known, is a story about stories. We have few original sources to tell us about his life, and the sources we do have are often contradictory or untrustworthy, so historians have had to piece together the story of Genghis Khan and fill in the blanks. What you will read here is a combination of historical fact, expert conjecture, and myths and legends, filtered through the changing eyes of history and retold through many generations. There are many things we simply do not know about the enigmatic figure of Genghis Khan. There are many things that we think we know that may ultimately prove to be untrue. What is important is the story. Just as the young Temüjin must have sat around a campfire to be regaled by stories of his ancestral wolf heritage, we now sit around this virtual campfire to share the story of Genghis Khan.

Chapter 1 – The Mongolian Steppe

Temüjin was a child who would go on to be a powerful uniting force, bringing together many different groups to create an almost unstoppable force under a strong, dominant leader. However, the world that he would shape was very different from the world he was born into. Far from being a unified empire, it was a world of warring factions where life was fraught with the danger of conflict.

Mongolia sits, as if being squeezed, between Russia and China. Extensive swathes of grassland cover much of the land, and the climate is one of extremes: long, cold, dry winters and brief, wet summers. Modern Mongolia is the world's second-largest landlocked country, and it has the sparsest population compared to its landmass. Around a third of Mongolian people are nomadic or semi-nomadic, a tradition that goes back to before the lifetime of Temüjin and the advent of the Mongol Empire.

In the 12th century, Mongolia had an almost exclusively nomadic population made up of many tribes. This was a time in human history where advances were being made rapidly in every aspect of civilization in many places around the world. In Europe around the time that Temüjin was born, the cornerstone of the great cathedral of Notre-Dame was laid in Paris. In England, Oxford University had been established. Huge social changes were happening at a speed never before seen in the history of the world, with great advancements in technology and trade that were transforming and expanding the known world. On the Mongolian steppe, also known as the Mongolian-Manchurian steppe, however, life continued much as it had for generations.

For the Mongols of the mid-12th century, life revolved around the struggle to survive in a harsh climate. The Mongolian landscape features very little arable land, so agriculture did not feature in the lives of these tribes. Instead, they made use of the wide grassy plains which provided grazing for livestock. Long winters and a short summer growing period meant that moving around was essential as the grazing pastures were quickly depleted. Life revolved around the herds and finding sufficient pastures for them to thrive. Without healthy animals, the Mongols would go without the essentials that made life on the tough Mongolian steppe possible. The herd provided them with animal hides, horns, meat, blood, milk, and a means for transportation.

It was a primitive life, and the traditional ways of doing things were important in making sense of the world around them. Life for the nomadic tribes on the Mongolian steppe was dominated by traditional practices. The family unit was the center of Mongol society, and one of the most important aspects of life was the planning of marriages, which would benefit the family and the wider clan. There were numerous family clans, related by blood and marriage, within a tribe, and marriage within the tribe itself helped to strengthen bonds. There was also intermarriage between different tribes, usually to secure an alliance between two tribes or as a result of kidnapping.

Temüjin's mother, Hoelun, had once belonged to another tribe called the Olkhunut. Despite her engagement to another man, she was kidnapped by Yesükhei and married to him. This was a common practice in Mongol tribes, and being selected as the chief wife of a man such as Yesükhei would have been considered a great honor for Hoelun. As the "chief wife," only the offspring of Hoelun could inherit, even though Yesükhei had at least one other wife that we know of who raised her children alongside Hoelun. Hoelun would go on to be hailed by literature as a great heroine of the Mongol people, a matriarchal figure that would come to be revered by generations thanks to her brave perseverance in the face of danger and her commitment to her son.

Nomadic life was difficult for the Borjigin tribe, especially in the harsh Mongolian climate. With no settled towns or villages, the nomadic tribes relied upon the *ger* for protection from the elements. A *ger* is a traditional yurt, built with a collapsible wooden frame. It is cylindrical in shape and covered in animal hides, lined with felt on the inside for insulation; much of the little warmth the Mongol people enjoyed came from the traditional felting of wool from their sheep to create a soft but durable dense fabric. A typical *ger* could be easily transported thanks to its light, compact construction, as it had to be erected quickly and taken down easily when it was time to move on. The tribe would move on for a number of reasons; for instance, they may have used up all the fresh grazing land for their livestock and had to seek new pastures, or they may have been forced to move on to avoid the threat of conflict. Seasonal changes would have also prompted the tribe to change location.

Wherever the tribe went, they relied on the land itself for all of their needs. Hunting and foraging provided them with sustenance, and keeping livestock was an essential part of their tradition. They reared sheep, goats, cattle, and camels for meat and milk, as well as for wool and hides for use in clothing and shelter building. Cattle and camels were used as beasts of burden to transport their belongings on the long journeys they would undertake when moving to a new area. Herds were large; for example, there were usually around 1,000 sheep in a flock, so they were often combined and herded together by multiple families working together.

The Mongol tribes also kept horses and were extremely competent horsemen. Horses were a tribe's most prized possessions and were used for food and for riding. Long hours were dedicated to the perfecting of riding skills and archery performed on horseback. Horses also provided sustenance; mare's milk was the main drink and was used to create a popular alcoholic drink, useful for keeping out the cold Mongolian winter. The blood of a horse could be used as emergency sustenance on a long journey by making an incision into the neck of the animal. It is well documented that the tough Mongol soldiers could survive with few supplies by drinking blood directly from the neck of their horses. The Mongol Empire that Temüjin would establish was founded on the horsemanship of the Mongol people. Without these amazing horses, there would have been no empire. Even today, the Mongolian people enjoy a reputation as some of the finest horsemen the world has ever seen.

The Mongol tribes lived mostly off the land but occasionally would trade some goods with the more settled peoples in the neighboring Chinese territories. At this time, there was no unified Chinese nation or country as we now think of it. Instead, there were a number of different dynasties which made up China. These dynasties were sometimes allied together and at other times opposed to one another. The Mongol tribes were often subdued by one or another of these Chinese dynasties—after all, it made sense to keep a close eye on these wild tribes to the north. The Chinese would encourage fighting between the Mongol tribes because tribes who were preoccupied fighting one another were much less of a threat to China. Sometimes, a tribe would gain power and make inroads into China while a particular dynasty's rule was weak, for example, when they were engaged in conflict elsewhere or dealing with political instability. Before long, the tribes would be pushed back again. This ongoing ebb and flow of power in which tribes would gain power and begin to expand only to be put back in their place by the Chinese dynasties had been the status quo for as long as living memory could stretch.

Aside from the ongoing conflict with their Chinese neighbors, the nomadic tribes themselves were engaged in a constant fight for dominance. Life was brutal; there was a lot of violence between rival tribes as well as the theft of precious resources as each tribe attempted to become the largest and strongest. However, even the largest and strongest of the tribes would not stay dominant for long, and there was a seemingly endless struggle to get to the top and stay there. The smaller and less dominant tribes were at risk of being obliterated, and the balance of power could change very rapidly, so as well as fighting with other tribes for survival, alliances were sought to secure mutual protection. The formation and breaking of alliances and the constant quest for revenge against enemy tribes, not forgetting the already tough nomadic lifestyle, made life incredibly difficult.

As if life wasn't dangerous enough, infighting within tribes was rife. Potential leaders attempted to assert their authority over their tribe, resulting in more violence and instability. With tribes themselves in constant flux and with the ongoing threat of annihilation from neighboring tribes, it is no wonder the nomadic tribes of Mongolia rarely made much progress in their attempt to gain land and power beyond the Mongolian steppe.

Temüjin, however, was born into a tribe and a family who remembered a time when they had had a taste of true power and when the tribes had once been united as one force.

Ancestral Legacy

Temüjin hailed from a long line of powerful leaders. His father was the leader of the Borjigin tribe and had many illustrious ancestors. His most famous forefather was undoubtedly his great-grandfather, Khabul Khan, also spelled as Kabul Khan.

Khabul Khan had been a daring leader who had managed to form a Mongol tribal alliance that went on to repel the invading Chinese Jin Dynasty when they attacked Mongol land. He famously tugged the beard of the Jin leader when he had been invited to the Jin palace, a great insult that gained him legendary status. Khabul escaped from the Jin and rallied an army to attack them. As a result, Khabul Khan became a heroic figure to many of the Mongols, and his direct descendants enjoyed a sense of nobility that helped them to stay on top and form good alliances to protect their privileged positions. This noble heritage would prove to be useful to Temüjin later in life as he sought to make connections and consolidate the Mongol tribes once again into a unified force, but it would be a long and arduous journey.

Ancestral legacy was particularly important to the Mongols for religious reasons. Tengrism, an ancient religion still practiced today, was followed by many of the tribes, and this belief system would help form the basis for Temüjin's personal beliefs as it advocated ancestral worship through connection with the spirit world. Honoring the ancestors was an important duty for every person, and Temüjin would have been raised to consider his ancestors to be very much a part of his experience of the world. This goes a long way to explaining the importance he placed on righting wrongs that he considered to have been committed against his family. As a son of the Borjigin leader, Temüjin inherited the rivalries and rifts of his father.

Religious or spiritual practice was a central tenet of Mongol life. The Borjigin were particularly affiliated with a sacred shrine on Burkhan Khaldun, one of the Khentii Mountains in northeastern Mongolia. This was believed to be the place where they had originated from. Despite a tumultuous childhood, this place and these beliefs were very important to Temüjin, and as an adult, he would return to his homeland after each campaign, often visiting the mountain, where he would fast and pray, placing offerings to signal his gratitude and meditating to seek guidance. As Genghis Khan, Temüjin would go on to become a semi-religious figure, himself a figure of veneration for followers of Tengrism for centuries to come. Many modern Mongolians view him with a semi-religious fervor and honor him with spiritual practices.

Temüjin would go on to have a profound impact on every aspect of the everyday lives of people in his home country and far beyond. From huge changes in how people lived their daily lives to sweeping reforms in how society itself functioned, right through to global change as the Silk Road was largely unified for the first time; thus allowing increased communication and trade between Europe, West Asia, and East Asia, this remote and primitive place, and this poor son of a petty chief, was about to change everything. In fact, if you know where to look, the effects of Temüjin's life and legacy can still be seen today.

Chapter 2 – Temüjin

While history has preserved the story of Temüjin's auspicious birth, there are few sources to tell us about his early years, and what information we do have is often contradictory. Many accounts of the childhood of the great Genghis Khan would have been invented to give him an impressive backstory befitting his later role as supreme leader. Much of the information we have about the leader comes from *The Secret History of the Mongols*. This mysterious text by an unknown writer is a rich source of information on the life of Genghis Khan, and it was written sometime after his death for the Mongol royal family. As such, we can assume that the information it contains is designed to be flattering to Genghis and the Mongols. This text is considered to be a classic piece of literature; it is highly prized by scholars and historians and is still taught to schoolchildren in Mongolia to this day.

What we do know is that Temüjin lived with his parents and six siblings; his brothers, Hasar, Hachiun, and Temüge, his sister, Temülen, and two half-brothers called Bekhter and Belgutei. Life for a nomadic child, even one who was a son of the leader of the tribe, would have been very tough. He would have been expected to learn quickly, to work hard, and to master valuable skills such as horsemanship, herding, and hunting. It is believed that Mongol tribal children would be tied securely onto horses from as young as three years old so that they could ride without falling off while learning to control the animal; a steep learning curve perhaps, but one that resulted in the expert horsemanship that came to characterize the Mongols.

To say that children in the Mongolian steppe were expected to grow up quickly by today's standards would be a huge understatement. There was no childhood as we think of it today. Life would have been unpredictable and fraught with danger; the tribes were entirely nomadic and regularly moved from place to place, sometimes unexpectedly, and political tensions between tribes often flared into violence. All we know of Temüjin's education is that his mother, Hoelun, taught him about Mongol society and the importance of forming alliances and building on ancestral achievements. This was a lesson that the young boy must have taken to heart, and it was quickly to become extremely important for his survival.

When Temüjin was around nine years old, he was taken by his father to the Khongirad tribe where a marriage had been arranged for him to a girl named Börte. The plan was that he would be put to work for his intended wife's tribe until he reached the accepted age for marriage, which was only twelve years old. This was standard practice among the nomadic tribes of Mongolia at the time; marriages between tribes were one of the few ways that they were able to maintain a balance of power, and so, children were often given in marriage to other tribes. By forging alliances through marriage and making gestures of goodwill such as the early delivery of Temüjin to the Khongirad, peace could prevail among the two tribes (for a little while anyway). Having been delivered to the Khongirad to embark upon his new life, Temüjin said goodbye to his father. Little did he know that he would never see him again.

Yesükhei's Death

On the homeward journey from the Khongirad tribe, Yesükhei encountered a group of Tatars. The Tatars were historic enemies of the Mongols and hailed from modern Russia, which is to the north of Mongolia. They were a fierce and powerful force, and clashes between the Tatars and other tribes were legendary. Yesükhei had long been in conflict with the Tatars. However, the Tatar tribesmen that Yesükhei encountered on this day asked him to join with them and sit down to eat together. This was an important and symbolic gesture of reconciliation, and so, Temüjin's father sat down with them in good faith. However, the gesture was a cruel trap. Yesükhei was given poison in his food, an act of revenge for his previous execution of Temüjin-üge, their chief, and he died soon after.

On hearing of his father's death, the courageous young Temüjin took charge of his future. Still a child at barely ten years old, he left his new home and returned to his own tribe where he expected to take his father's place as leader. Instead, he found that the tribe had expelled his mother Hoelun and her other children, along with his father's other wife and children. This may have happened for many reasons. Firstly, Temüjin was considered too young to become the head of the Borjigin, but more importantly, this was a good opportunity for the rival Tayichi'ut family to seize control and lead the tribe. Perhaps the tribe was not willing to support the former leader's widows and children, especially if those children could grow up to become rivals for power. Whatever the reason, Hoelun and her children were abandoned and forced to live in extreme poverty. Their herd, the key to their livelihood, had been stolen by other members of the tribe, leaving them destitute.

Hoelun is described in *The Secret History of the Mongols* as running along the riverbanks, searching for nuts, fruits, and roots to feed her children, a testament to her tenacious nature. Foraging was her only means of providing for the group of young children. It was a far cry from the rich diet they would have been accustomed to as part of the tribe, who dined on mutton, horsemeat, and mare's milk. She relied heavily upon Temüjin for help. Ostracized from the community he had grown up in and at odds with the new Tayichi'ut leadership, Temüjin found himself with the sudden responsibility of feeding and protecting a family without the security of the tribe. He asserted himself as leader of the family, and they hunted, fished, foraged, and kept sheep in order to survive. Hoelun instilled in Temüjin a sense of his importance in the world and a passionate determination to avenge both his father's death and the loss of his rightful role in the tribe. Temüjin and Hoelun had a close relationship, whether from necessity for survival or from a fondness between them we will never know, but even when Temüjin was at the height of his power as Genghis Khan, he delegated responsibilities and took advice from his mother, even placing children belonging to defeated enemies into her capable care.

Despite their difficult circumstances, Temüjin held fast to his authority over the group. Before long, he felt that his unofficial leadership was being threatened by his half-brother Bekhter, who was considering superseding Temüjin by marrying Hoelun (who was not his biological mother). This would have been a common occurrence among tribes; a man would often have left one of his wives to one of his unrelated sons. Temüjin was not willing to be superseded by another member of the family, however. Tension mounted until Temüjin murdered Bekhter on a hunting trip after a dispute about how the spoils of the hunt should be divided. Temüjin had sent an important message to his extended family; his authority was not to be questioned.

Temüjin, the Slave

Life was full of constant threats, and this came not just from the elements and the fight for survival, but it also came from their fellow Mongols. When he was around fifteen years old, Temüjin was captured by the Tayichi'ut. Rather than killing him, they kept him as a slave for over a year, imprisoning him and fastening him by the neck using a type of wooden collar that functioned in a similar way to stocks. Temüjin bided his time, patiently waiting for an opportunity to escape. One night, when the tribe was distracted by feasting and frolicking, he managed to knock his guard over by using the heavy collar as a weapon. He ran from his captives. Temüjin had finally escaped the clutches of the rival tribe, an impressive feat for a boy so young. He must have been a precious prisoner, as he was both a strong, powerful young man and a symbol of the old ruling family who the Tayichi'ut had usurped. They certainly did not want to lose him, so he was pursued by the tribe through the night. One famous story tells that when Temüjin was found by a member of the Tayichi'ut, the captor was compelled by the tenacious fire in

Temüjin's eyes to help him escape, putting his own life at risk by doing so. Clearly, the noble Borjigin family still commanded respect from the tribespeople, despite their fractioned past. Temüjin hid in a river crevasse, and then later, when it was safe, he escaped back to the relative safety of his family.

In 1178, finally free from slavery and again dominant over the family group, Temüjin married Börte. This was the woman his father had always intended him to marry, and this secured his alliance with the Khongirad tribe. Throughout his life, Börte remained his wife, and although he had many other wives, as was customary in Mongol society, she was his only empress. It was only his children from Börte who were able to inherit his titles and powers, placing her in a very privileged position. Some sources suggest that Genghis Khan had as many as five hundred wives (and many more concubines) as he collected new wives while he traveled across his rapidly expanding empire.

Soon after their marriage, Börte was captured by the Merkit people. They kidnapped her and married her off to one of their own tribesmen as a symbolic act of revenge because Temüjin's father, Yesükhei, had kidnapped Hoelun from the Merkit people and married her. Such acts of revenge commonly occurred even a generation after the initial insult as the Mongol people did not easily forgive such transgressions. Temüjin himself was legendary for his ability to hold onto a grudge until he could avenge it. By this point, Temüjin was already beginning to build up a following of loyal men, but the kidnapping of his wife accelerated his plans. He began to rally his friends and allies to embark on a daring mission to rescue Börte. Calling on allies of his father and friends of his youth, they fought the Merkit tribe, and against the odds, they triumphed. This was the foundation of an army of allies that would come to be one of the most notorious and successful military forces ever established.

After her rescue, Börte soon gave birth to a son, Jochi, and despite the uncertainty of the child's true parentage, Temüjin accepted the child as his own. He went on to have three more sons with Börte: Chagatai (1183–1242), Ögedei (1186–1241),   and Tolui (1191–

1232), as well as an unknown number of daughters. He had many other children with his other wives and concubines, so the exact number of his offspring can only be guessed at. Mongol culture advocated the birth of many children, and one of the things that Genghis Khan is most associated with, in the popular mindset, is the spawning of thousands of offspring.

The young Temüjin is an intriguing character. For a man still in his youth, he appears—at least from the sources that we have on him—to have been incredibly strong-willed, resourceful, and determined. We know little of his personality other than what we can guess from his early actions. The few other facts we have about him give us little insight; we know he had a passion for falconry and would go on to indulge this hobby throughout his life, employing eight hundred servants to look after his eight hundred falcons. He was rumored to have a fear of dogs and to be partial to a bottle of Shiraz.

Still in his formative years, with the weight of his ancestors pushing him ever forward, Temüjin forged relationships with other tribes and continued to call upon old allies of his family. His thoughts returned to seeking revenge for his father's death and claiming his rightful position as a powerful leader. Temüjin's legacy, both biological and military, had only just begun.

Chapter 3 – Becoming Genghis Khan

Temüjin's formative years had been incredibly difficult. He had been surrounded by danger from the moment of his birth and had managed to not only survive, protect his family outside the tribal community, escape slavery, and rescue his young wife, but he had also managed to maintain the respect that his father's name commanded and built alliances with other tribes.

His most important ally at this time was Toghril, his father's *anda*. Toghril was also known as Wang Khan or Ong Khan, a Chinese title similar to "king." *Anda*s in Mongol society were blood brothers, close friends who had sworn to support and honor one another until death. It was a sacred duty that should never be shirked. Toghril was the ruler of the Kerait tribe and one of the most powerful and wealthy of all the Mongol tribal leaders. He had large armies at his disposal, and after first coming to Temüjin's aid when rescuing Börte, he became a close ally. The reason for this alliance owes much to the fact that Toghril was a close ally of his father, but he also sought vengeance on the Merkit tribe, who had abducted Börte, for his own reasons. Toghril himself had once been abducted and used as a slave by the Merkit. However, his level of trust and respect for the son of his *anda* seems to have gone far beyond a sense of duty. He promised to help Temüjin to reunite his tribe and provided a large army of over twenty thousand men, a very generous gesture on his part, especially to such a relatively inexperienced man with no real power of his own. The balance of power between the two was so unequal that historians have puzzled over Toghril's commitment to the young warrior, who had nothing to offer in return but a sable skin that he had received as a gift following his wedding as a gesture of thanks and respect.

Temüjin's Charismatic Power

Toghril's surprising sponsorship of Temüjin is one of a number of examples that suggest that Temüjin had an almost supernatural ability to gain the respect and admiration of people wherever he went. Another great example of this amazing ability to gain followers and supporters is found in a story about stolen horses. When Temüjin's struggling family group was living as outcasts from the tribe, they had their horses stolen. This was a serious loss—horses were essential to life for Mongol nomads. Temüjin was determined to track down the thieves and asked a farmer along the roadside if he had seen anything. This farmer's name was Bo'orchu, and he was so impressed by Temüjin and the natural authority that emanated from him that not only did he give him a fresh horse and help him to find the thieves, but he also abandoned his own family and swore allegiance to Temüjin, becoming his *nökör*. A *nökör* (comrade) in Mongol tradition is a companion who has completely devoted his life to the service of a leader to the exclusion of everything else. This was the first recorded *nökör* of Genghis Khan, but many of the generals who served under him turned their backs on families and personal lives in order to fully dedicate themselves to Genghis Khan.

Sworn Friends Become Mortal Enemies

Temüjin also received help in his earliest military days from Jamukha of the Jadaran tribe. Jamukha had been a boyhood friend of Temüjin, and he was persuaded by Toghril to contribute an army to help Temüjin in his quest to reunite his tribe and seek revenge on the Tatars. Although Jamukha started out as an ally, the two leaders soon found that their beliefs in how Mongolia should be governed were irreconcilably different.

Jamukha believed in the traditional Mongol transfer of power through families, an aristocratic system where rulers came from the ruling families who had always held power. Temüjin believed in a meritocracy. He strongly felt that leaders should gain their positions by earning them and being well suited to the job, and one of the reasons why his military was so successful was his habit of choosing the most talented leaders regardless of their status or family.

Jamukha and Temüjin, once friends, became enemies. Jamukha felt threatened by the speed with which Temüjin was gaining power. He had watched as Temüjin had formed alliances with many of the Mongol tribes and saw him becoming increasingly popular. In the year 1186, Temüjin was elected as Khan of the Mongols—the leader of all the Mongol people. He was not yet given the title Genghis Khan. Before he received that honor, he would have to prove himself by uniting all the tribes of the Mongolian steppe and defeating all those who opposed him.

Gathering together 30,000 soldiers, Jamukha attacked Temüjin's forces in what would become known as the Battle of Dalan Balzhut in 1187. Jamukha was successful in the battle, but this was not a total defeat for Temüjin. Jamukha dealt mercilessly with those he defeated; news that he had put to death a group of seventy captives by boiling them alive, among other acts of cruelty, turned many of the Mongol tribesmen against him and led them to support Temüjin. Despite this popular support, Temüjin had lost power as a result of the defeat, and his protector, Toghril, was exiled. While historians don't have a lot of evidence for what Temüjin did for the next few years, it is very likely that he was garnering support and training the men loyal to him in his newly devised military tactics. This often involved getting rid of the aristocratic rulers and training common men as workers and soldiers, gaining him further popular support from the tribespeople.

Revenge on the Tatars

It was around 1197 when Temüjin finally got the opportunity to avenge his father's death. This was an important turning point in the young man's life. This was a chance to have his revenge on those who tricked and murdered his father. It was also an opportunity to gain power and recognition as a military leader.

The Jin or Jurchen dynasty, a Tungusic dynasty who ruled over much of northeastern China and Manchuria, requested an alliance to fight the Tartar army. Temüjin, along with a number of other tribes including that of his father's *anda*, Toghril, was to play a pivotal role in the battle. He was placed in command of part of the attacking force when they went up against the Tatars and dramatically defeated their armies, resulting in a heroic success. In a famous order that was to become almost a signature move, Temüjin commanded that every Tatar male who was taller than the linchpin of a wagon wheel would be put to death. Those who were shorter, presumably children under three feet tall, were taken into his care. Temüjin's brutality on the battlefield often contrasted with his commands that the tribespeople of the tribes he defeated be absorbed into his own rapidly growing tribe. Those who were not killed were cared for, and in this way, Temüjin was able to quickly gain admiration from new followers, soldiers, and servants who were loyal and committed to his aims. Those who were not suitable for integration were wiped out. It was this policy that helped to lead to the rapid growth of the Mongol Empire.

Once the Tatars had been defeated, Temüjin and Toghril were honored by the Jin and found much of their former power restored to how it had been before their defeat by Jamukha. Temüjin found himself in a stronger position than he had ever been in before. His reputation as a fierce warrior, military strategist, and ruthless leader preceded him; it was the perfect time to surge forward and take control of the warring Mongol tribes once and for all.

The Unification of the Tribes

Temüjin had the support of the three most powerful Mongol tribes, but despite his successes and his popularity, there were still some major tribes and many smaller ones who did not align themselves with him. Old rivalries and different political ideas surrounding the debate over whether an aristocratic or meritocratic approach should be taken meant that Temüjin had a seemingly impossible task ahead if he was ever to unite the tribes. The various nomadic tribes had never been fully united under one leadership. Their shared history was one of violence, vengeance, and the constant vying for more power.

However, Temüjin was not doing things the old way. He could see that true power would only come from unity. By turning his back on the Mongol traditions that had held the collective tribes back from fulfilling their potential and developing new strategies that rewarded loyalty, he gave the common people opportunities to thrive based on their hard work and merit. He was, in turn, rewarded with a dedicated army that he could then train in his revolutionary new military techniques that set them apart from every enemy they encountered. Each tribe they defeated swelled both their numbers and their coffers. Traditionally, soldiers were expected to hand over anything they looted to be shared among the aristocracy. Soldiers in Temüjin's army could keep much of the spoils of their looting, provided that no looting took place until the enemy was thoroughly defeated and the looting had been permitted. This opportunity to benefit financially was no doubt a keen motivating factor. It was no accident that Temüjin allowed his soldiers to reap personal financial rewards in return for complete success on the battlefield; this policy was key to his wider success.

Naturally, the rival tribes were increasingly concerned by Temüjin's dominance. Even Toghril's tribe, one of Temüjin's key allies, became threatened by his power. It was around this time that Toghril's son, Senggum, convinced his father to break their close alliance. Toghril was initially reluctant—after all, his alliance with

Temüjin had been instrumental in restoring his power—but as time passed and Temüjin's power only grew, the relationship between them soured. This was finally confirmed when Toghril refused to give his daughter to Temüjin's firstborn son, Jochi. In Mongol culture, this was a great insult. This mark of disrespect was quickly followed by Toghril's strategic alliance with Jamukha, who by now was one of Temüjin's keenest enemies. Together they planned assassination plots to rid them of Temüjin for good.

It wasn't a good move for Toghril, and this severing of his friendship with Temüjin would soon lead to his downfall. In 1201, Jamukha was elected to the position of "universal leader" by a *kurultai* (a tribal assembly of all the Mongols)—a move that set him up as the leader of all the remaining tribes who had not already been defeated by Temüjin or defected to his rule by choice. This was a move that should have united the remaining tribes under a singular leadership with a common enemy, but instead, it only served to fracture the already strained relationship between Jamukha and Toghril. They were rapidly losing the trust of their allies, and the dispute between them was too much for the alliance to bear.

Toghril attempted to form a coalition with other tribes in order to oppose Jamukha, but Temüjin's armies defeated this combined force. After the battle, Toghril was killed by another tribe as he fled the conflict. Toghril did not have the honor of dying in battle; instead, he was murdered because the tribe who came across him simply didn't recognize him. It was the beginning of a rapid decline for Toghril's Kerait tribe.

The tribe who found and killed Toghril were known as the Naimans, and as sworn enemies of Temüjin, they took in Jamukha and his remaining followers. However, despite Jamukha's attempts to rally support to rise up against Temüjin, many of the Naimans eventually defected as Temüjin continued to defeat and absorb rival tribes, becoming a massive, unrelenting force that swept through the land. There was still some fierce resistance, but Jamukha's commitment to his political ideals of class status proved to be his ultimate undoing. Unlike Temüjin, he refused to recruit common men such as shepherds and those without tribal status. Instead, he stuck rigidly to the ideals of the aristocracy. It was only a matter of time before Temüjin gained the upper hand and scattered Jamukha's armies. In 1206, Jamukha, the "universal leader," was handed over to Temüjin, betrayed by some of his own men who had switched allegiances.

The Death of Jamukha

The story of how Temüjin dealt with his deepest rival, the boyhood friend of his childhood who had become his nemesis, has become legend. Instead of welcoming the gesture of the men who delivered his mortal enemy to him, Temüjin had them put to death, refusing to have them in his armies because they had been so disloyal to their leader. For Temüjin, betrayal of the leader was the ultimate transgression, even if it resulted in him being handed his enemy on a plate.

Jamukha was not killed by Temüjin right away. Despite having been one of his most ferocious opponents, Temüjin offered him the opportunity to renew their friendship and reestablish the bond they had once had in their youth. Jamukha refused the gesture, announcing that there was only room for one sun in the sky and only room for one Mongol lord. He was allowed to choose the method of his own execution and requested that he have his back broken rather than his blood spilled. This was a Mongol custom and allowed Jamukha to achieve an honorable death. He was also given a decent burial, wearing the golden belt that Temüjin had given him in their younger years, long before their bitter rivalry had taken hold.

Genghis Khan

Having done something that no man had ever done, subduing or claiming victory over all of the Mongol tribes, Temüjin secured a peace agreement. In 1206, tribal leaders came together to honor Temüjin with the title of Genghis Khan. The title means "Oceanic Ruler of the Universe," more commonly translated as "Universal Ruler." Temüjin had indeed become the universal ruler of Mongolia, but this was much more than an honorary title. It was a new identity.

This new identity had its basis not in politics but in religion. The religion of the Mongol people, Tengrism, was a shamanic practice. When the most important shaman announced that Genghis Khan was a representative of the chief god himself, Möngke Koko Tengri, the Eternal Blue Sky or Heavenly Father, the transformation of Temüjin was complete. No longer was he considered to be a mere human. He had been transformed in the eyes of the Mongol people into a spiritual leader as well as a great military and political force. Having unified the Mongols, he turned his attention to the wider world, and so began the incredibly rapid growth of the Mongol Empire. We will never know how Temüjin felt about his new status, but the weight of the expectations of him cannot have been lost on him. We do know that he took his role as being the representative of god on earth extremely seriously, resulting in one of his most famous quotes: "I am the flail of God. If you had not committed great sins, God would not have sent a punishment like me upon you."

Chapter 4 – Building the Mongol Empire

Turning his attention to the world beyond his home country, Genghis used the might of his well-trained military forces to begin the expansion of the Mongol Empire. Buoyed up by the success he had already had in uniting the tribes of the Mongolian steppe and considering himself to be divinely inspired by predictions of his victory, Genghis began to plan. His ultimate aim was to defeat those who opposed him and gain territory, and his most famous quote gives us some idea of the pleasure he took in defeating his enemies: "The greatest happiness is to vanquish your enemies, to chase them before you, to rob them of their wealth, to see those dear to them bathed in tears, to clasp to your bosom their wives and daughters."

There were many neighboring factions which the Mongols had old grievances with, and as we know, Genghis was not a man to forget a grudge. Many of his early actions in expanding the Mongol Empire were attempts to wreak vengeance on old enemies, in much the same way that his earliest military actions were against tribes such as the Tatars who had killed his father. Vengeance was to become a recurring theme in the life of Genghis Khan, and he backed up his vengeful ambitions with skilled military and precision planning. The combination of motivation, fierce determination, and expert skill was to prove deadly for the population of Central Asia.

The Xi Xia

Genghis Khan's first campaign in his wider quest to expand the Mongol Empire outward into the world was against the Xi Xia, or Western Xia kingdom. Also known as the Tangut Empire after the Tangut people, who were of Sino-Tibetan origin, the Xi Xia was part of what is now northwestern China. The Xi Xia territory bordered the Mongol Empire and had long since been an intimidating enemy. Genghis needed to conquer a vassal state, a state that would be submissive to him and could provide valuable tribute and military support. The Xi Xia was an ideal candidate for such a vassal state; it was wealthy, influential, and close to the Mongol homeland.

The conquest of the Xi Xia began somewhat tentatively. There was a long tradition of the nomadic tribes of the Mongolian steppe making forays into this territory to conduct raids and fight minor battles. Genghis' armies began with a series of these raids, possibly to create fear or to get some idea of what they would be up against should they choose to launch a larger battle campaign. These raids on the border regions of Xi Xia had been happening since before Genghis was proclaimed universal leader, so this was merely an increase in what had been a long campaign of attrition. During one of these raids, the son of a Xi Xia commander was captured by a Mongol army and taken into their service. He grew up within the army under the new Mongol name of Chagaan and was eventually promoted to be the head of Genghis Khan's personal guard. This is one of many examples of one-time enemies being incorporated into the Mongol army, often into positions of authority. This gave Genghis a wider pool of men to choose his most skilled commanders from, as well as giving him vital inside information about the culture and inner workings of enemy states. Having an enemy with a high status defect to his army also helped him to command loyalty from those he conquered and often encouraged them to submit without the need for conquering!

The results of these raids must have been promising because, in 1209, a major invasion took place. The invasion made use of two of the Mongol army's favorite tactics to great effect. The first was to send in large numbers of mounted archers, cavalrymen with finely honed archery skills who were able to cover distances quickly and fire on the move. This enabled them to reach the city of Yinchuan. The second tactic that sealed their success at Yinchuan was a false withdrawal. This gave the enemy false hope that Genghis' men were retreating and enabled the Mongols to turn back and use the element of surprise to successfully bring the city under siege.

The plan was to flood the entire city, forcing the people to surrender. The flood attempt didn't go to plan as the river that Genghis' army diverted unexpectedly flowed back and flooded the Mongol camp. Despite the disastrous mistake, it was still enough to force the emperor of the Xi Xia, Li Anquan, to surrender and submit to the invading Mongols, offering a tribute to secure peace. The emperor of the Xi Xia submitted to vassal status, serving the Mongol Empire and providing tribute. The Xi Xia provided military support when Genghis went to war with the Jin dynasty, who had refused to send help when the Xi Xia were under threat from the Mongol Empire.

However, the Xi Xia later tried to break their alliance with the Mongols, waiting until Genghis was preoccupied with the war in the east against the Khwarazmian dynasty and then taking their chance to break away from the empire. This audacious attempt was a great insult to Genghis Khan, and he angrily sent his armies into Xi Xia with orders to massacre the population and sack the towns and cities. The capital was again put under siege, and although Genghis would not live to see it, it eventually fell in 1227, and the Mongol armies massacred the people of the city and took complete control of the Xi Xia territory.

The Mongol-Jin War

Once the Xi Xia had submitted to vassal status, Genghis had a strong supporting force, which meant he could confidently turn his attention to the Jin dynasty. This was the beginning of the Mongol-Jin War, and it would last from 1211 until 1234. The Jin dynasty, led by the

Jurchens, controlled a large area in what is now northern China. The formation of a unified Mongol Empire was a huge threat to the Jin, who benefitted from the infighting amongst the individual tribes as it prevented them from ever mounting a serious attack on Jin territories. There was a history of hatred between the Jin and the Mongols; they had been determined enemies back in the time of Khabul Khan, Genghis Khan's ancestor who had tried to unite the Mongol tribes. For a long time, the Jin dynasty had demanded tributes from many of the neighboring nomadic tribes on the Mongolian steppe, punishing them with raids and attacks. Many Mongol people were killed or kidnapped to be used as slaves for the Jin. The Jin Jurchens had aligned themselves with the Tatars and Keraits against Genghis, with the aim of conquering the tribes.

The Mongol-Jin War began with an insult when a new Jin leader came to power. Wanyan Yongji sent diplomats to demand that Genghis submit to the Jin, effectively meaning that the Mongol Empire would become a vassal state to the Jin. Genghis reacted by turning to face the south and spitting on the ground before riding off in the opposite direction. This was a grave insult to the diplomats, and from this point on, a war which had seemed likely was completely inevitable.

However, Genghis did not rush to attack the Jin. Even though he had been approached by high-ranking Jin officials who had defected and encouraged him to attack, he was reluctant. He decided to practice caution in case he was being led into a trap. He formed a *kurultai* and sought political and military advice at great length and detail. The story of Genghis seeking divine approval for his war with the Jin tells that he made his way into the mountains where he prayed and asked for guidance. After days on the mountain, he returned and announced that he had been promised a victory against the Jin and that he would surely have vengeance for the many wrongs the Jin had committed against the Mongols.

The war began in 1211, and in the early days, the Mongol armies conducted minor but targeted raids. They destroyed food supplies and wreaked havoc on the rural population, but they did not massacre the people. Instead, they were working tactically to devastate the land so that the people of the country would be forced to run to the cities. The larger towns and cities were flooded with refugees seeking shelter and food, putting pressure on their resources and—just as importantly—spreading fear of the ferocious army of Genghis Khan. The refugees brought little with them other than the stories of the terrifying and brutal Mongol forces. Genghis Khan had learned that an enemy's fear was one of the most powerful weapons that he could use against them. Soon, there was a shortage of food, and the cities couldn't take in any more refugees.

At this time, the Mongol armies began to attack on a larger scale. They used defectors from the Jin to secure a safe route and get inside information into the Jin defenses. Using their innovative military techniques, most notably their ability to move fast while fighting, they were able to secure victories over each army that the Jin sent to battle. The Mongol army was able to spread out, creating a multi-pronged attack that helped gain them territory. In 1213, the Mongol army attacked the capital, Zhongdu, the city now known as Beijing. With the city under siege, the Jin agreed to submit and made a generous tribute to Genghis' Mongol Empire, including silk, precious metals, and horses, as well as the presentation of a princess to Genghis. Far from securing peace, this was only enough to secure a temporary lull in the hostilities.

Cracks were starting to appear in the Jin leadership, as the emperor and his generals disagreed about how to defend the dynasty. When the generals wanted to attack the retreating Mongols, the emperor refused and instead moved the capital to Kaifeng, which was more secure. Genghis viewed this move as a betrayal of their agreement, and it wasn't long before the Mongol armies were on the attack again, reinforced by defecting Jin armies. Zhongdu was all but destroyed, and the Mongol armies set about bringing the rest of the Jin territory under control. While the Jin continued to fight, they were always defending rather than attacking, and the Mongol armies were both persistent and strategically superior. After over 23 years of fighting, the Mongols won the Mongol-Jin War, giving them control over a vast, wealthy province rich in resources and with a valuable source of food in the extensive rice fields.

Qara Khitai

After Genghis Khan had conquered the Jin dynasty, the reputation of his armies preceded him, and he found that other territories, such as the Uyghur Buddhist Qocho Kingdom, would surrender before the Mongols had even threatened them. Many smaller provinces and those without allies submitted willingly and joined the Mongol Empire. The Mongol Empire was growing outward in all directions, and the next natural step was to gain control of Qara Khitai, or the Western Liao dynasty, a province that extended westward from Mongolia to the Aral Sea. Again, Genghis could recount a number of perceived wrongdoings that justified revenge against the Qara Khitai. It was also the key to expanding westward across Central Asia toward Europe.

When Genghis had defeated the Naimans and united the Mongol tribes in 1206, the Naiman leader, Kuchlug, had fled and taken refuge with the Qara Khitai. He married into the ruling family and became a respected military commander before seizing power for himself in 1211. He now had control of a huge territory, but he was proving to be a deeply unpopular leader. While Genghis Khan was promoting religious tolerance, Kuchlug had converted to Buddhism and then forced his largely Muslim population to convert to either Buddhism or Christianity. Genghis Khan's forces had been involved in intense conflicts for many years at this stage, and they were exhausted. To invade the Qara Khitai would require a very different tactical approach, and so, Genghis set about inflaming the mounting civil unrest, inciting dissent and turning Kuchlug's supporters against him.

Kuchlug then made another fatal error; he attacked the Karluks, a vassal state of the Mongol Empire. The Karluks promptly called upon the empire for help, which was delivered swiftly in the form of twenty thousand skilled soldiers who easily liberated the Karluks and then made their way to the Qara Khitai capital. In the capital, they were faced with thirty thousand of Kuchlug's soldiers.

However, Genghis' forces had one of his most skilled generals in charge—Jebe, known as "the arrow." Despite being outnumbered, Jebe secured a heroic victory against the Qara Khitai. Kuchlug managed to escape, but Jebe's men pursued him, and he was captured by hunters who delivered him to the empire's forces. Kuchlug was beheaded, a bloody death that the Mongols would have considered being a dishonorable, even shameful, way to go. The conquest of Qara Khitai took just two years, from 1216 until 1218, and yet it secured an important part of Central Asia and gave the Mongol Empire a border with the Khwarazmian Empire, which was—conveniently—precisely where Genghis saw his empire expanding next.

Khwarazmian Empire

The Khwarazmian Empire extended across most of modern Iran, Turkmenistan, and Uzbekistan, as well as large parts of Afghanistan, Kyrgyzstan, Tajikistan, and southern Kazakhstan, and it was a largely Muslim state ruled over by Shah Ala ad-Din Muhammad II. There were many reasons for Genghis to covet the Khwarazmian Empire, but the biggest one was the potential trade links it could offer. The Silk Road, the most extensive trade route, would give the Mongol Empire the perfect opportunity to trade valuable goods with Khwarazmia. Genghis extended the offer of trade, saying, "I am master of the lands of the rising sun while you rule those of the setting sun. Let us conclude a firm treaty of friendship and peace." In an attempt to form an official trade agreement, the Mongol Empire sent a large caravan of tradeable goods to the Khwarazmians. Perhaps the reputation of the Mongols went before them, in a more negative way this time, because the caravan was attacked by a suspicious Khwarazmian governor, Inalchuq, who took it to be a cover for a spying mission.

Genghis responded to this attack by sending Mongol diplomats, accompanied by a Muslim envoy, to talk to the shah. The shah responded with violence, shaving the Mongols (this would have been considered a grave insult) and sending them back to Genghis carrying the severed head of the Muslim envoy. This gesture was designed to cause serious insult to Genghis and his empire; the shah wanted Genghis to know that his attempts at diplomacy would always be completely rejected. The Mongol Empire was not just unable to trade with the Khwarazmians, but it was also becoming clear that it was under threat from the Khwarazmian Empire, who were proving increasingly hostile.

Genghis responded by plotting his most ambitious battle plan yet. He raised an army of over one hundred thousand soldiers—who were now experienced and battle-hardy—and assigned them generals from his most trusted and skilled military commanders. Perhaps even more telling, he made his own personal preparations to go into battle against the Khwarazmians by announcing his successors. By setting his affairs in order before he set off, Genghis was protecting his empire and preparing himself and his family for the possibility that he would sacrifice himself for it.

The Mongol attack on the Khwarazmian Empire was a complex one. Making use of information obtained by spies, Genghis' soldiers divided up into three large armies which attacked the Khwarazmians first in the northeast. Then Jebe's army secretly moved to the southeast while Genghis himself attacked from the northwest. Using three large forces to surround the enemy was an intelligent approach to invading a country which had many small armies stationed in various towns and cities because any escaping soldiers from their minor armies would be driven toward the oncoming path of another Mongol army as they moved in. The shah's policy of dividing his armies up meant that the Mongol forces could basically sweep across the land, disposing of each small army as they came to it. There was no large unified force to defeat, and so, progress was made quite quickly.

The city governor Inalchuq, who had insulted Genghis with the severed head of his envoy, came to a violent end and gave the world one of its most lasting stories about Genghis Khan. He was killed by having molten silver poured into his eyes and ears. The shah was not to be spared either; Genghis sent his generals to track him down and kill him after hearing that he had fled his court. On reaching a settlement, the Mongol army would massacre the citizens, although evidence suggests they were lenient toward craftspeople and skilled workers, who were sent back to Mongolia where they could work. All soldiers and aristocrats were slaughtered, and the people who were spared from the massacre in the towns were driven forward in front of the army to the next settlement where they would function as a human shield, protecting the Mongol army from any defensive attacks mounted by the Khwarazmians. The citizens who had escaped death were taken as slaves or absorbed into the Mongol army.

The conquest of the Khwarazmian Empire supplied history with many of the most brutal stories associated with Genghis Khan. Towns and cities were destroyed, agricultural land was devastated, promises of leniency if cities surrendered were often betrayed, and there was looting, burning, and pillaging almost everywhere that the Mongol armies went. It was after the defeat of Khwarazmia that travelers described great mountains of human skulls along the landscape, built as a monument to the Mongols' victory or as a warning to would-be rebels. In one particularly bloody battle at Urgench, the death toll amounted to around 1.2 million people, making this one of the most violent and devastating conflicts in world history.

While stories of the death toll and the gruesome and barbaric violence perpetrated by the Mongol armies is likely to have been part of a publicity campaign by the Mongols to ensure that future enemies were more likely to submit to them rather than stand up to them, there is no doubt that it was a bloody conflict. Spreading terror among their foes was one of the most effective tactics that the Mongols developed, as it enabled them to avoid actual battle as often as possible; yet when a battle was necessary, they were merciless. The Khwarazmian population was devastated by the Mongol invasion.

Further Expansion

After the devastation of the Khwarazmian Empire, Genghis led his army back to Mongolia through modern-day Afghanistan and India, where they raided and pillaged the settlements they reached as they made their way home. A larger army, led by trusted commanders Jebe and Subutai, went on an epic journey through modern-day Armenia, Azerbaijan, Georgia, Crimea, and Russia. While there are few good sources of historically accurate information about this quest, evidence suggests that it was an incredibly successful mission, and the Mongol Empire had soon expanded to include the territories that Jebe and Subutai passed through. Despite unfamiliar terrain, difficult climates, and being greatly outnumbered (at one point facing eighty thousand enemy soldiers with just twenty thousand of their own men), the Mongol forces were victorious.

The Mongol Empire was even able to conquer Russia, and historians often point out that this is something both Napoleon and the Nazis failed to do. Experts suggest that a large part of the Mongol success in Russia came down to the hardy Mongol horses and the Mongol soldiers being used to harsh conditions. The Russians did attempt to secure a peace deal with the Mongols, but this was rejected, and the Russian princes who had extended the offer of peace were executed. Stories of the executions of the princes became legendary; Subutai ordered them to lie on the ground and then had a large wooden platform placed on top of them. The generals feasted on this platform as the princes were slowly crushed to death underneath them.

The campaign of Jebe and Subutai spread the word of Mongol military prowess into Europe. When the Mongol forces returned to Mongolia in 1225—with Jebe dying along the way—the Mongol Empire was thriving, gaining the upper hand against the Jin, and enjoying a reputation that made it practically immune to attacks. Life in the empire had also changed, and Genghis Khan had made sure that while the Mongol Empire expanded, the citizens were not forgotten. He set about righting what he believed to be wrong with society and installing a strict set of laws to keep order in the empire.

Chapter 5 – Life in Genghis Khan's Empire

Genghis Khan aimed to continue to expand his dominion beyond the traditional territories of the tribes. The Mongol tribespeople under his rule numbered over one million, so he already had considerable power, and now his empire was growing at an incredible rate. If his turbulent childhood and rise to power had taught him anything, it was that firm control was required if he was to stop the united tribes from descending again into warring factions. If he wanted to be able to spread his empire out further, he needed stability, peace, and prosperity at home.

To maintain peace among the tribes, Genghis made sweeping changes to life for the Mongols. He promoted social equality by removing the titles of aristocrats and giving positions of power to those who showed an aptitude for leadership and loyalty to the universal leader. By getting rid of the old titles and positions of authority, and replacing them with his own trusted generals, he eliminated the risk of any tribe rising up against him. He also made sure that his armies were not formed from solely one tribe, mixing the soldiers so that there were representatives of different classes, backgrounds, and tribes in each group so that their common link was their loyalty to him and to the Mongol Empire.

Genghis Khan also set in place structures and rules that would encourage peace and prosperity for the Mongols. While the widespread slaughter of those who resisted was common, for those who submitted or survived, life under Genghis' leadership was relatively peaceful. This was largely due to a code of practice known as the Yassa.

The Yassa

The Yassa code began as a series of rules and practices for use during wartime. The clever—if somewhat unfair—thing about the Yassa was that it was not made public. By keeping the rules secret, they could be changed and used in whatever way suited Genghis and the leaders he put in place. There is no complete copy of the Yassa laws, so, unfortunately, we do not have a definitive list, but there are extracts and references to them in other existing documents which give us some insight into the laws of the Mongol Empire. Lots of these laws were later adopted by other regimes as well.

The basic tenets of the Yassa laws were absolute loyalty and obedience to the rule of the universal leader, the unity of the Mongol tribes, and the acceptance that anyone found guilty of doing wrong would be punished harshly. Even the most minor of misdemeanors would receive merciless punishment; famous examples include the death penalty for a soldier who failed to pick up something that another soldier in front of him had dropped or a hunter who allowed an animal to escape from a community hunt. By setting in place harsh punishments and then following them up with swift action, people were controlled through fearful respect. They would certainly benefit from the protection that the Yassa code offered them but only if they toed the line and followed the rules. It was a delicate balance, but one which resulted in a much more stable everyday life for ordinary citizens.

The Yassa in Everyday Life

The Yassa laws governed how people lived day to day. It acknowledged the existence of one true god but protected many from religious persecution and encouraged religious tolerance. It protected people from the theft of property and kidnappings with harsh punishments and the threat of death for thieves. Community values were enshrined, for example, making it compulsory to share food and drink with a passing stranger without them asking.

There were rules for hunting, as it was forbidden to kill certain animals during breeding seasons so that a great hunt could be held each winter to exercise the soldiers. Rules about slaughter and preparing food gave detailed instructions forbidding the cutting of an animal's throat and instead insisting that the abdomen of the animal be cut open and the heart squeezed by one's hand until the animal was dead. That being said, sometimes the law was rather brutal toward religious minorities, such as Muslims or Jews, and forbade them, on pain of death, from practicing their religious customary slaughtering techniques such as *dhabihah* and *shechita*, respectively. Water should be drawn with a suitable vessel and not scooped with hands. If you offered food to another person, you had to taste it yourself first, regardless of any disparity of status between the two people eating. For instance, a noble would have to taste the food of a captive. Food should be shared equally, with no one person permitted to eat more than anyone else, and nothing could be eaten without it first being offered to everyone present.

Many rules guided people on how to treat captives. These were essentially slaves taken from populations which had resisted the empire. No Mongol person was to be taken as a captive or a slave. An escaped captive had to be returned to their captor and could not be fed or given clothing until the captor had given permission. This made it practically impossible for a captive to successfully escape. Perhaps this was something Genghis Khan had learned when he himself had been aided in his escape from captivity.

Rules on marriage, inheritance laws, and the treatment of women changed the traditional practice of the Mongol people by giving legitimacy to the children of concubines, making them eligible for inheritance. Adultery and sodomy were both punishable by death. The sexual assault of women was also a crime punishable by death. Women were given more freedoms than previously had been allowed; Genghis even permitted his wives to join him at the table to eat, and they were allowed to speak and share their opinions. In a time when women were granted little in the way of rights, this was a big step forward. Some accounts of the Mongol Empire talk about the sisters and daughters of Genghis Khan being given de facto powers. This was accomplished quite deviously by giving the official role as local leader to the woman's husband and then ensuring that he was either kept busy as far away as possible fighting in the army or, even better, conveniently killed in battle, leaving the woman to make the decisions.

The Yassa laws laid down how society was to be conducted. It ensured that no one was granted power without being elected by a Mongol council. The poorest in society were protected from poverty, and religious leaders, monks, and certain other professions were exempt from paying taxes under the Yassa rules. Titles were forbidden—everyone should be referred to using their own name, even Genghis Khan himself. Sorcery, purposeful lying, treachery, and deceit were all to be punished severely, and people were expected to conduct themselves honorably at all times.

The Yassa laws were overseen by Genghis himself and members of his family who he had chosen to ensure that it was carried out correctly. The threat of punishment was not an idle one; Genghis understood that the fear of punishment was a major factor in controlling the people in his empire, and this became more and more important as the Mongol Empire grew, but he also knew that this fear could only be generated by ensuring that the punishments dealt were swift and merciless.

While many of the Yassa laws were designed to result in a fairer society, there is evidence that how stringently the rules were applied also depended on who you were and whether or not you were in favor with Genghis Khan. Those who Genghis particularly liked were often given many "second chances."

Many of the rules and punishments might seem entirely baffling to modern people. For instance, children who had died could be married in order for two families to form an alliance, it was against the law to wash clothing or one's body in running water during a thunderstorm, and urinating in water or ashes was deemed worthy of being put to death! While some of these seemingly insignificant actions were crimes you could be killed for, murder was less of an issue—you could have simply paid a fine in gold or donkeys to exonerate yourself.

Righting Societal "Wrongs"

Genghis improved life for the Mongol people in practical, tangible ways by implementing the Yassa laws that made previously common practices illegal. These new rules directly related to the experiences that Temüjin had as a young man. No longer was it deemed acceptable to enslave another Mongol person, nor was the practice of kidnapping or selling women permitted. Property was to be respected, and the sentence for the theft of another family's livestock was death. He had experienced the devastation caused by infighting between tribes, losing his own father and his community due to it. He had been a slave and suffered. His wife had been kidnapped and taken from him. His family's horses had been stolen. He understood the elements of Mongol life that caused distress to the individual and damage to the wider community. It does seem that Genghis was righting what he viewed as the "wrongs" in his society based on his own experiences, setting in place barriers that would prevent anyone else from rising up as he had. Eliminating these threats to social stability not only improved the sense of security and therefore the quality of life that people enjoyed, but it also gave their leader secure power over them.

Religion

Genghis Khan's religious beliefs were rooted in traditional Mongol Tengrism, a religion that incorporates elements of shamanism, animism, and ancestor worship. Tengrism is centered on the belief that the earth and everything in it were created by a heavenly spirit of the sky who rules over the world. The blue-sky spirit and the earth spirit cater to the needs of the people on earth. Tengrism is still practiced today in Mongolia and other Central Asian countries.

While Genghis Khan's role as the universal leader was dependent on the assertion by shamans that he was the living embodiment of the blue-sky spirit, Genghis himself was remarkably tolerant of alternative religious viewpoints. While he may have a reputation as the world's most notorious warmonger, he did not fight religious wars. We know that Genghis Khan was a spiritual thinker; he was particularly superstitious and is often described as praying or going off to seek spiritual clarity. He actively encouraged the preservation of local traditions and religious practices, and he went even further than this, seeking out religious, philosophical, and moral instructions from lots of different sources, including spiritual advisors, shamans, and astrology experts. In his later years, he would command a Taoist alchemist to create him a potion—an elixir of life—so that he might live forever.

As the Mongol Empire spread, Genghis encountered a wide range of different philosophies and religions. He embraced this opportunity to learn and is known to have consulted religious leaders from other traditions, including Buddhists, Muslims, Christians, and Taoists. Religious debates were encouraged in the empire, with public debates between leaders becoming a great source of public entertainment.

Genghis Khan's embrace of diversity and his role as a defender of religious freedom has been a constant source of wonder to students of history. However, the Mongol Empire benefitted in two main ways from this tolerant stance. Firstly, this allowed people to hold on to most of their beliefs even after they had been defeated and dominated by the Mongols, which made them more accepting of the new regime. Secondly, Genghis was able to reach out to those who were oppressed for religious reasons in other nations and use them as spies and usurpers, promising them religious freedom when their home nation was taken over by the Mongol Empire. This religious tolerance was instrumental in the success of the empire, and many years later, when religious tolerance declined, the empire followed suit.

The Yassa in the Military

The Yassa laws also described how soldiers should behave and what was expected of them. No soldier was allowed to leave his post or defect, and the first priority of every soldier should be his absolute, unquestionable loyalty to Genghis Khan. Every Mongol man was expected to be available for battle, and if a man did not go to war, which would have been permitted in exceptional circumstances only, then he was expected to offer free labor for the good of the empire. Often this meant providing a service that benefitted the army, such as making weapons or armor. Life in the army was tough, but the soldiers were well rewarded for good behavior in accordance with the Yassa. Mongol life became dominated by the servicing of its vast army, including its training, supplies, and campaigns.

Chapter 6 – Military Genius

Genghis Khan's early success and the rapid expansion of his Mongol Empire was largely a result of his military acumen. The Mongol armies were different from anything the world had seen before. They were organized differently, they fought differently, and they had different ideas. The generals placed in positions of command by Genghis Khan were men who had earned their power rather than men from a particular family. By giving important military roles to those who were most deserving, Genghis had ensured that his armies were led by intelligent men who would have the skills to adapt to circumstances and learn from experience.

As the Mongol Empire spread across Central Asia, the Mongol armies were able to take advantage of the technology and innovative techniques employed by the people they conquered. As they gained experience of many types of warfare, they were able to develop strategies that would work against any enemy they encountered.

Military Strategy

Genghis Khan was undoubtedly a great military strategist. He took into consideration what the enemy was thinking, basing his actions on how he anticipated the enemy would react. While there are plenty of stories that suggest he acted in anger, retaliating for insults and taking disproportionate vengeance, there is no suggestion that this anger led him to make irrational decisions. In fact, all of his military campaigns were very much based on logic, strategy, and thorough knowledge of his enemies' motivations. Battle strategy was a priority for Genghis, and he developed plans of attack that were often extremely complicated. For each battle, he would carefully weigh the risks and potential gains of engaging with the enemy before he attacked. He was not afraid to withdraw if he felt the risks outweighed the benefits and would hold back until he could be reasonably sure of victory. While he was by all accounts a brave fighter, Genghis himself would often withdraw and hide from the battle itself. He had a personal guard of 10,000 elite soldiers to protect him, but his role as the leader of the Mongol Empire and the motivating force of the armies made him a prize target and too precious a leader to risk losing in battle.

Intelligence and Espionage

One of the ways that Genghis ensured that he was making good strategic choices was by establishing a network of spies who gathered intelligence that would help guide his battle tactics. These spies were sent into an area in disguise to create maps that would show travel routes and useful resources as well as taking note of defenses and any other relevant inside information. This intelligence could be passed on quickly using a fast relay messenger system.

Genghis' spies also served another purpose. Disguised as travelers or traders, they were able to tell the local people tales of where they had been and what they had seen. This was an ideal opportunity to spread terrifying stories about the Mongol forces in order to create fear and unease within the population. Exaggerated stories about the atrocities committed or heroic tales about cities who had submitted and been treated with mercy by the Mongols could quickly spread through a community, and this had a profound effect on how the local people saw the Mongols and thus how they reacted when the Mongols approached.

Loyal Soldiers

The soldiers themselves were a highly organized and disciplined force. Every man in the Mongol Empire was automatically a soldier; there was little choice in the matter. The soldiers were intensively trained in horsemanship, weaponry, and battle tactics. Genghis used a massive annual hunting festival to train the soldiers, which was why hunting of certain animals was forbidden during the breeding season to allow greater numbers of animals for this annual hunt.

Perhaps the most important quality in a soldier, in the eyes of the universal leader, was loyalty. Genghis demanded absolute loyalty from his soldiers, and he achieved it through a mixture of fear—disloyalty was punishable by death—and incentive—loyalty was rewarded. In return for loyal service, soldiers were given a share of the bounty from looted enemy settlements, and they were treated relatively well. The armies were well supplied by a complex supply system that kept them well-fed and armed. Spiritual guidance and medical attention were provided by shamans who accompanied the army. Family life was entirely possible, with huge caravans of nomadic families following the armies.

The Cavalry

The key to understanding the Mongol army and how it differed to other armies of the time lies in understanding the role of the cavalry. The Mongol army was mostly made up of cavalry, but instead of the heavy cavalry seen in other armies such as the European knights, the majority of these were light cavalry who relied upon speed, mobility, and excellent archery skills to rain down arrows on the enemy and quickly change direction to evade an attack.

The Mongol light cavalry was highly trained in complex maneuvers. They used stirrups and gripped the horse with their legs so that they could fire arrows while riding at full speed. They were famed for their ability to fire arrows in all directions, including behind them. These soldiers were expert archers, timing each shot to precisely the split second when all four of the horses' legs were off the ground to get a smooth shot.

The horses used by the Mongols were exceptionally well suited to life in the Mongol army, and the success of the Mongol Empire owed a lot to the small but perfectly formed Mongol horse. Mongol horses were happy to graze and forage, so no grain was needed to feed them, making it easier to travel long journeys without the need for supplies. They were hardy and could handle low temperatures, which gave the Mongols an advantage when fighting in tough conditions during winter, especially in Russia. Each soldier had a number of horses so he could always be sure of having a fresh, healthy horse on long journeys or when faced with unexpected combat.

Horses held an almost sacred role in Mongol life. They were protected by extensive armor, and when a soldier died, it was not uncommon for his horse to be sacrificed so that they would remain together in the hereafter.

Contrary to popular belief, nearly four out of ten Mongol soldiers were heavy cavalry. Heavy cavalry generally carried lances and blades, which allowed them to attack in close combat after the light cavalry archers had broken up the enemy's lines of defense. The combination of a highly mobile light cavalry and a well-armed heavy cavalry behind proved to be deadly.

Decimal Military Divisions

Genghis revolutionized how armies were divided up. Instead of forming armies based on the status or tribe of the soldiers, he had very strict ideas about how an army should be formed. Units of ten men were formed. These were known as an *arban*, and they contained men from different tribal backgrounds and of different social status. A company of one hundred men was known as a *jaghun*, one thousand men formed a *mingghan*, and ten thousand men made up a *tumen*. This meant that each soldier lived within a small family unit with nine other soldiers, with no man higher than another. This expectation of equality meant that each man could prove himself based on his loyalty and military achievements rather than relying on his birth or name to progress through the ranks. A census was arranged so that every man would be counted and expected to fight. Armies could quickly be assembled from multiple *tumens*, creating large armies of as many as a hundred thousand soldiers. Armies this size, moving across the wide expanse of grassland with the families of the soldiers, their animals, and the supplies they would need, must have been an incredible sight to behold.

Psychological Warfare

Genghis Khan used psychological warfare to great effect, and this is partly why it is difficult for historians to get a realistic picture of the Mongol Empire. It is likely that stories of battles were greatly exaggerated in order to generate fear; Genghis preferred his enemies to submit willingly, and they were much more likely to do this if they believed that the Mongol forces were even more terrifying and merciless than they were.

Psychological tactics were also used in battle. These tactics included making the army look and sound larger than it was. Dummies would be placed on the backs of horses to give the impression of more riders, bonfires would be lit to make the nighttime camp look more extensive, and lots of noise was generated using drums. Demoralizing the enemy with shows of strength, silent attacks followed by deafening drum beats accompanying coordinated charges, and intimidating siege weaponry helped win the psychological battle before the Mongols had even engaged in battle.

Inclusion

One of the tactics that stands out the most when looking at Genghis Khan's military strategy is the policy of absorbing enemies into his own army. Subjugated enemies who submitted and were deemed worthy of inclusion in the Mongol army were spared death and joined the ranks of the army. Perhaps a mixture of gratitude, fear, and self-preservation transformed these one-time enemies into loyal soldiers, but perhaps the legendary charisma of Genghis himself and the quasi-religious fervor of his supporters converted those he had conquered.

The most compelling story of inclusion, and one that is often used to demonstrate the complex thought process of Genghis Khan, is that of Jebe. Jebe, originally named Jirqo'adai (Zurgadai in modern Mongolian), was an enemy soldier who fought against Genghis during his campaign to unify the tribes. During a battle, Genghis was wounded. After the battle was over, he asked his attendant to find out who had injured his horse (because it simply wouldn't do to admit that he himself was the target of the arrow). Zurgadai voluntarily confessed that it was he who had shot the arrow. His bravery and honesty impressed Genghis. Zurgadai went on to say that Genghis could kill him if he wanted, but if he spared his life, he would be a faithful and loyal servant. Genghis was so enthralled with Zurgadai that he renamed him Jebe, a Mongol name which means arrow, and gave him a position in his army. Jebe turned out to be a master military strategist, and he won many important campaigns for Genghis, whom he served faithfully as he had promised.

Uniform and Equipment

Soldiers wore a uniform designed for the harsh climate. Underneath a heavy robe, they wore a tight silk undergarment that offered added protection from arrows (and made it easier to remove any arrows that did manage to pierce the skin). On top of this, the Mongol soldier would have worn extensive lamellar armor. This armor was essentially a type of chainmail made up of many small scales for flexibility. The distinctive helmets worn by the Mongols were cone-shaped and often decorated with horsehair. The armor and helmet of a soldier may have been made from metal or from hardened leather, depending on their rank.

The Mongol army had high expectations of its soldiers; as well as partaking in rigorous training, the men were expected to maintain their equipment and take care of up to five horses. Each man had to carry tools, supplies, food, and clothing in large saddlebags. These saddlebags were inflatable and doubled as flotation devices for crossing rivers.

Weapons

The Mongol soldiers had a wide range of weapons at their disposal. Each soldier would have most likely had a bow and arrows, a shield for defense, a lasso, and a dagger or sword, usually strapped to the left arm. These weapons developed over time, and many of them were influenced by other cultures that they encountered as the empire spread. Genghis was quick to adopt the technological developments he came across.

The Mongol Bow

By far the most important weapon of the Mongol army was the composite Mongol bow. These incredible weapons were made from wood with a layer of horn on the inner side and sinew on the outer side. This gave the bow the perfect balance of tension and compression so that it had an excellent range as well as incredible precision.

Each archer would have had more than one bow, and each would have worn a quiver which contained around sixty arrows, with extra quivers carried by camels who were stationed nearby so that archers could restock quickly. A large number of arrows was needed because each archer would fire successive shots, reloading in seconds and attacking quickly so that the enemy would be rained upon by a shower of arrows. It is estimated that the Mongol bow could shoot an arrow with a maximum range somewhere between 1,300 and 1,600 feet (400 to 500 meters), an astonishing distance compared to other weapons of the time.

As part of the campaign of psychological warfare, arrows were developed which would inflict maximum injury rather than kill outright, others were designed to make a piercing whistling sound when flying through the air, and others were dipped in flammable liquids and ignited before being fired, causing panic and setting settlements alight.

Siege Weaponry

Siege weaponry was extremely important if Genghis' armies were to penetrate heavily defended settlements. The Mongols, remember, had always been nomads, and so, they were unaccustomed to the difficulties posed by the walls and defenses of towns and cities. As we have seen, Genghis was keen to take up the technology he encountered on his travels outside of his home territory. He purposely spared engineers and builders of weaponry so that he could benefit from their skills and put them to good use developing new technology for the Mongol army to use. Campaigns in China and Persia resulted in many new ideas for siege weaponry, such as trebuchets and mangonels. By taking engineers with the army,

Genghis' men didn't have to drag heavy siege equipment and machinery to the scene of the battle. Instead, he ensured they recruited the very best engineers who could build efficient siege weaponry on site.

Bombs

Surprisingly, the Mongols did have explosives, and it is thought that they were some of the earliest armies to utilize gunpowder. Cannons, explosive bombs, and possibly even early Chinese firearms may have also been used. This technology was in its infancy at the time, but the Mongols may have encountered the secret of gunpowder in China and used it to add to their already impressive repertoire of weaponry.

Battle Tactics

Military historians are extremely interested in working out how the armies of Genghis Khan were able to decimate the population and conquer such vast swathes of foreign territory, often against armies that were many times larger than the Mongol forces. When an army is severely outnumbered, as was often the case for the Mongol armies, a lot rests on the battle tactics employed in the field.

Communication

On the battlefield, communication was essential. Communicating complex orders to a large army that was often spread out to make it appear even larger than it was proved to be a challenge. To do this effectively, the Mongol armies used smoke signals, drumbeats, and flags to communicate and coordinate orders during battles. It is even believed that the Mongols may have invented an early form of semaphore. Intensive training ensured that every soldier was familiar with the orders being communicated so the whole army could move as one man, improving agility, which was crucial to many of the military maneuvers that made the Mongols so successful. Leaders and strategists positioned on hills nearby would literally oversee the battle and use this perspective to give complex orders.

Agility

Agility and mobility were what set the Mongol army apart from other armies. There were a number of factors that made them able to move more quickly and change direction so rapidly. First of all, there was the standard of their horsemanship, which was taught from an early age and which armies trained in intensively. This was made easier by the nature of the horses themselves, as they were smaller, lighter, and known for their agility.

Broad Front

The Mongol army tended to form a broad front with cavalry archers at the front followed by heavier cavalry. The broad front was deep, but it was also agile, so it could change direction easily, confusing the enemy and diverting them into a position that suited the Mongols before attacking in order to minimize losses on the Mongol side. After the archers had rained down thousands of arrows on the enemy and the enemy's front lines were broken up, the heavier cavalry would surge through and attack in close combat using lances and blades.

Coordinated Attacks

Complex techniques usually required great coordination, which was why communication and organization into decimal units were so important. Battle tactics, such as encircling tactics, which was when troops would split up and encircle the enemy army or settlement to attack from all sides, overwhelming the enemy, won many victories. Hit-and-run attacks sent high impact attacks into the enemy forces; the Mongol soldiers would then withdraw to avoid casualties before regrouping and attacking again. Wave tactics sent waves of troops swarming the enemy, causing disorientation and panic. Knowing when to use each of these powerful tactics was the job of the commanders who were chosen from the most experienced and successful of the soldiers.

Feigned Retreat

The Mongol army mastered the difficult art of feigned retreat and became notorious for this highly effective tactic. To do this, they would pretend they were retreating, acting as though they were under threat and panicking before turning and beating a hasty retreat to safety. When the enemy, thinking that they were winning the battle, pursued them, often breaking out of formation and spreading out as they did so, the Mongols would turn and destroy the enemy troops. Even after they had become famous for this technique, the Mongols still continued to use it, drawing out the time they spent in a feigned retreat for long enough to convince the enemy, patiently pretending they were losing for days, or even weeks, before attacking with deadly force.

The Element of Surprise

Ambush attacks were a common feature of Mongol campaigns. Genghis understood that to surprise an army when they were unprepared meant an easier victory, and he used this to great effect. Scouts and outriders would give intelligence back to the Mongol forces, who would then plot elaborate ambushes where the enemy would be surrounded and overwhelmed. The Mongol armies also used the scouts and outriders to track enemy movements so that they themselves could avoid surprise attacks, making them notoriously difficult to ambush.

Siege Warfare

Siege warfare was a learned skill for the most nomadic native Mongols, but it was common in other territories, and they were keen to embrace powerful siege weapon technology. Surrounding a settlement until the people starved, redirecting rivers so that settlements flooded, and terrifying the enemy with displays of strength, loud music, and generally being extremely intimidating was all part of winning the psychological battle when a settlement was under siege. The Mongols were inventive and resourceful, firing containers of oil, flaming missiles, human and animal corpses, rocks, and wood. Engineers on the battlefield gave the army new and useful options; machines could be built to fire missiles, water could be crossed using rafts and pontoons, gates and walls could be battered with battering rams, giant ladders could be erected to scale fortifications, and huge stockades could be built to protect the Mongols from enemy missiles. Any problems that arose could be solved by the engineers in a way that soldiers could not have managed alone.

Chapter 7 – Innovation

The early days of Genghis Khan's rule were a time of rapid social change and development. Everything had changed for the tribal peoples of Mongolia, and while Genghis Khan was expanding his empire by rapid military action, he did not turn his back on life at home. New laws and rules had been implemented, but Genghis was also deeply involved with the process of developing new technology, systems, and ways to make life easier. These innovations had a lasting impact, and many of them underpin aspects of the modern world; we are all still affected by the changes that took place under Genghis Khan back in the 13th century.

As the Mongol Empire spread, the Mongols encountered new innovations and technologies from other places. Not only was this great for the military, which benefitted from better weapons and new tactics, but it was also revolutionary for the people of the empire, who were able to adopt and adapt new ideas. From a new universal currency using paper money to agricultural development, trade, writing, and even an early postal service, the Mongol Empire was a hive of innovation.

Money

Just as Genghis unified the tribes, he also set about replacing local currencies with one Mongol currency. When he first came to power, there were many different types of currency, from bronze coins to silver pieces to a traditional bartering system where goods of one type were simply swapped for another type. When the tribes had been frequently warring with one another and were at risk from neighboring ruling dynasties, trade had been fraught with difficulties. Now that the tribes were unified under one all-powerful leader and infighting was strictly forbidden, there was a growing feeling of security. Security allowed trade to flourish, and so, currency became a more pressing concern than it had been before.

Genghis set in motion changes in the currency system which continued to evolve throughout his own lifetime and beyond. He is widely credited with spreading the concept of paper money. While paper money had been used in China prior to Genghis' rule, the Mongol Empire can be credited with taking this relatively new concept and spreading it across the continent.

Marco Polo, the famous Italian explorer and writer, visited the Mongol Empire when it was under the rule of Genghis' grandson, Kublai Khan. Marco Polo was shocked to discover that the currency used was, in fact, made of paper. He famously reported that the Mongol Empire was forged using "might, force and the bark of trees." Marco's astonishment at a government-backed currency, rather than private currency, resulted in a detailed explanation of exactly how this system worked, right down to how the money itself was made. His stories amazed the Western world.

In *The Travels of Marco Polo*, Marco describes their process of making money as a kind of alchemy.

> He makes them take of the bark of a certain tree, in fact of the Mulberry Tree, the leaves of which are the food of the silkworms—these trees being so numerous that whole districts are full of them. What they take is a certain fine white bast or skin which lies between the wood of the tree and the thick outer bark, and this they make into something resembling sheets of paper, but black. When these sheets have been prepared they are cut up into pieces of different sizes.

He was astounded that the khan was able to use such a seemingly simple system of producing paper to essentially ensure that he owned everything, making him the richest man on earth:

> With these pieces of paper, made as I have described, he causes all payments on his own account to be made; and he makes them to pass current universally over all his kingdoms and provinces and territories, and whithersoever his power and sovereignty extends. And nobody, however important he may think himself, dares to refuse them on pain of death. And indeed everybody takes them readily, for wheresoever a person may go throughout the Great Kaan's dominions he shall find these pieces of paper current, and shall be able to transact all sales and purchases of goods by means of them just as well as if they were coins of pure gold. And all the while they are so light that ten bezants' worth does not weigh one golden bezant.

Marco also discusses how this new innovative currency impacted trade. When merchants arrived in the Mongol Empire, they were not allowed to trade precious metals or gemstones freely; they must sell to the emperor. To do this, the value of the goods was assessed by an expert who then gave the trader a good price in the form of paper money. They could then take this paper money and buy anything they wanted from anywhere in the empire. This was an appealing deal to the traders and an even better one for the khan. As Marco pointed out, it cost him nothing to issue the paper money, saying, "whilst all the time the money he pays away costs him nothing at all."

This system of currency, which essentially meant that all wealth belonged to the khan and yet which promoted trade and encouraged industry, was a key factor in the growth of the empire, yet it could not persist indefinitely; such a system would eventually suffer from inflation and instability. Later leaders would attempt to reinstate a multi-currency system without success.

Written Language

There was no writing system among the Mongol people before the Uyghur Qocho Kingdom peacefully surrendered to Genghis Khan, and he commissioned a writing system similar to the Uyghur alphabet. It seems that Genghis was a great believer in literacy and promoted reading and writing among the people. There were other writing systems across Asia, but none of them were particularly suited to the Mongol language. The Uyghur script was not ideal either, but it was the first step toward an efficient system of writing, and it introduced the concept of writing to a large number of people to whom the idea was completely new.

Kublai Khan, Genghis' grandson, would build on the legacy of his grandfather by commissioning a Tibetan man called Drogön Chögyal Phagpa to create a whole new written language. The idea of this language was to establish a new method of writing that would be extended throughout the defeated lands which had been incorporated into the empire. It became known as "square script," and while it was used on official documents, legal papers, and money, it never properly caught on among the people themselves. So, while the Mongol Empire might never have quite achieved a written language that was adopted universally, it did have a huge impact on the literacy of individual people, promoting written language where there was none before.

Agriculture

The Mongols had been nomadic and were fiercely proud of their nomadic heritage before the rise of Genghis Khan as the universal leader. Once the tribes had been unified, they continued to live a nomadic lifestyle, hunting and foraging for food as well as keeping livestock. The diet of the Mongol people was based around two food types—the red foods, which were meat, and the white foods, which were milk-based. The few plants that made it into their diet came from foraging rather than cultivating crops.

While the climate of Mongolia was not amenable to planting crops, the expansion of the empire coincided with a change in climate, as there was a phase of more temperate weather that made life easier for the Mongol people and encouraged early forays into agriculture. Other parts of the Mongol Empire, where the land and climate were better suited to planting and harvesting, saw a boost in agricultural activity. Genghis Khan himself was a late convert to the idea that agriculture could lead to a stronger economy, but when he became convinced that settling down and planting the land could be a more prosperous way of life than nomadism, he encouraged it.

Again, these early seeds of agriculture (so to speak) were watered by Kublai Khan, who encouraged schemes to get peasant people farming the land. Farming was considered to be excellent work for the lower classes; not only did it make them productive members of society, but it also produced larger amounts of food. Food security was a big issue, and agriculture offered a viable solution. As an added bonus, excess food could be traded, helping to bring in more money, which was always useful for expanding the empire further.

Örtöö

One of the earliest innovations established by Genghis Khan was a system of passing messages, and even now, this system is hailed as one of the earliest successful postal systems in the world. The Örtöö (commonly known as Yam in most Western languages) was a system of relay stations used by messengers. To send a message, one of these messengers, who would have been a skilled, efficient horseman who could cover great distances very quickly, would make their way as fast as possible to an Örtöö station. The message would be passed to a fresh messenger who would then take it to the next station in the manner of a relay. This meant that there was no delay in sending a message or a document; it could travel at top speed without the need for stopping because a messenger or horse needed to rest.

There were many Örtöö stations, with often just twenty to forty miles between them. Each station was equipped with fresh horses, food, and supplies, as well as offering shelter to messengers who could then rest up for their next assignment. The result was an incredibly efficient messaging system. The success of Genghis' armies owed a lot to the Örtöö messengers who were able to reach even swiftly moving armies with important information. This meant that valuable time was saved, and the armies were able to learn of the latest developments much more quickly, allowing them to surge into battle when necessary and hold back when deemed wise. The faster the commanding generals were able to get hold of new information, the faster they could react to it, and this made the armies much more efficient. It was especially useful when conveying information gained through espionage, something that Genghis used a lot to give him insight into his enemies' activities.

This messenger system was something Genghis believed very strongly in, and there were much investment and refining of the Örtöö to ensure that it was as fast and efficient as it could be. The Yassa laws protected those who ran the stations and conveyed the messages, giving them privileges and compelling citizens to help with the smooth running of the Örtöö whenever necessary. Each messenger wore a special metal pendant known as a *paiza*. This was a form of identification that proved their importance and status as messengers.

The Örtöö, which was initially free for merchants to use, later became a source of income for the empire, as anyone wishing to use the service, other than those in the service of the khan, had to pay a fee. This Örtöö system was the most expansive and well-organized messenger system that the world had ever seen, and it was marveled at by travelers who reported on the speed and efficiency with which information was able to flow across the huge empire.

The military innovations that enabled Genghis Khan and his successors to build the Mongol Empire are well documented, yet the innovations that took place outside of the military are just as essential in understanding how the great expansion of the Mongol Empire was possible. Without currency, trade could not have flourished in the way it did. Without the Örtöö, the armies would never have been so successful. Without a writing system, the laws would have been much harder to enforce. Without agriculture, everyday life would not have been as stable. Genghis understood the need to back up military might with stability at home—people needed to be fed, and they would be happier and less likely to rebel if they had a decent quality of life where they felt like they were living better than they had in the past.

Innovative developments not only helped society to thrive, but they also helped Genghis Khan to command loyalty and devotion from his people.

Chapter 8 - Death and Succession

While there is some debate over the year when Temüjin, later and better known as Genghis Khan, was born, we have a much more precise date for the day that he died. We know that on August 18th, 1227, the ruler of the Mongol Empire passed away. He would have been around 65 years old and was still taking a very active role in both military command and the leadership of the Mongol Empire at the time of his death.

The passing of Genghis Khan came at a very critical time in a campaign to end troublesome uprisings in China. The Xi Xia dynasty was making a brave attempt to end the rule of the Mongol Empire in their former territory and restore the old dynasty to power. Having already subdued and conquered the Xi Xia once, Genghis retaliated with brutal force. This was a common response from Genghis and his generals when subjugated enemies attempted to rise up again and resist the Mongol Empire; while Genghis rewarded loyalty well, he also mercilessly punished disloyalty and resistance. If he might have spared some of the population when first conquering a territory, they could be certain that if he had to return and subdue them again, they would not be.

Whether Genghis Khan had a death that would have been considered noble and fitting to the Mongols is a question that no one can truly answer. The truth has been lost to history, and there are many different stories that seek to describe how and where he died.

We have the rather mundane version of events in which he succumbed to a respiratory disease such as pneumonia. Diseases like this would have been relatively common, and infections spread easily among soldiers in close quarters. Genghis was relatively old at this point and was under pressure to regain the Chinese territories, so illness is not unlikely.

There is another simple explanation that he was killed in battle against the Xi Xia or that he died later from wounds caused by an arrow. We know that Genghis often avoided taking part in the battle directly, and when he did, he was surrounded by a large guard force of thousands of men, so a direct hit in battle seems unlikely. However, if the leader was suffering from illness and fatigue, he may have chosen to die honorably in battle rather than succumbing to illness or disease.

Then there is the more fanciful story that he was stabbed by a stolen princess. Genghis is said to have had a dream of blood on a bed of white snow. His shaman interpreted the blood as being that of a Xi Xia prince who would die in battle and the snow symbolic of a pure princess who would never accept any of the men who attempted to woo her. Genghis is said to have seen the death of the prince and had taken the princess to bed. To prevent her rape, the princess took a dagger that she had hidden on her person and attempted to castrate him. In this version of events, Genghis died of blood loss. This account was recorded long after the death of Genghis and originated from an enemy tribe who was possibly trying to invent a story to dishonor him, so it is less likely to be true.

Experts cannot agree which of the sources that talk of Genghis' death is the more reliable, but the most plausible and commonly repeated version of events is that he fell from his horse while on a hunting expedition and was gravely injured, dying later from his injuries. This version of the death of the khan is recorded in *The*

Secret History of the Mongols and includes the suggestion that after his fall, he succumbed to a feverish illness, which may be the respiratory condition that some other sources speak of.

Whichever of the stories is true, Genghis was certainly an old man by the standards of the time, and the fact that he was still leading troops into battle is a testament to his strength and determination as a ruler. News of his death was kept a secret from his troops and from the enemy. Understandably, they could not allow news of the leader's death to spread. The soldiers viewed Genghis as a legendary, almost immortal figure, and word that he was dead would be seriously damaging to morale. The Xi Xia, on the other hand, would certainly rejoice in the news, and this could have given them the edge in battle. On his deathbed, Genghis Khan gave the order that the entire Xi Xia were to be killed in punishment for rising up against the great Mongol Empire. Soon afterward, the uprising had been put down, and the Xi Xia were practically wiped out. After a time, it was deemed safe to announce that Genghis was gone.

Ögedei Khan, the Successor

Living a dangerous life (to say the least), and well aware of the rivalry that would spring up among his sons and relations after his passing, Genghis had long since announced that his successor was to be his son, Ögedei. The reason Ögedei was chosen as the next Great Khan instead of Jochi, who was the eldest, was to stop Genghis' sons from contesting the succession. There had always been some doubt over the parentage of Jochi, as he had been born just months after Genghis' wife had been rescued from another tribe. Genghis had accepted the baby boy as his own son, but the question mark over his heritage would have been enough to cause potentially devastating conflict between the other legitimate sons. Ögedei was seen as a safe pair of hands for the empire; he had fewer quarrels with the other relatives and was a capable leader.

The property of Genghis Khan was divided out among his sons and other relations; Genghis' wealth lay mainly in his armies, and there were around 130,000 men to be passed on as an inheritance. They were the source of Genghis' power, and so, passing control of these men was symbolic of passing along his power. It was traditional in Mongol culture that the youngest son received the father's property, and so, Tolui received 100,000 men. Most of the remaining men were divided up among his other sons and his brothers, with a few being left to his mother's relatives and his wider family circle.

Stories of Genghis' material wealth vary. While he is believed to have looted vast quantities of bejeweled gold objects, decorated weaponry, and religious artifacts from the territories he conquered, he claimed to practice asceticism, reportedly claiming that he ate the same food and dressed in the "same rags" as his herdsmen.

Realizing that the Mongol Empire was too large for one ruler and desiring for his sons to inherit with as little tension or cause for conflict as possible, Genghis Khan also designated khanates, which were sub-territories that would be managed independently by minor khans who would be loyal to the Great Khan. He gave his sons these khanates, and essentially, this was the beginning of the division of the Mongol Empire into separate states. The same squabbling and infighting among the aristocracy that Genghis had done away with in order to unite the tribes was a threat to his own family, and without the strong presence of Genghis to keep the peace among his own sons and grandsons, the empire was at risk from descending into chaos.

The Burial of Genghis Khan

Just as he had announced his successor long before his death, Genghis had also expressed his wishes regarding where he was to be buried. And yet, this is possibly the greatest mystery of all. Historians, archaeologists, and the governments of China and Mongolia cannot agree on where and how Genghis was interred, and while there have been some very tantalizing hints, theories, and clues about where he may lie, a grave has never been found and confirmed to be that of Genghis Khan.

What we do know about the burial of Genghis Khan is that it was also kept secret at the time. It was Mongol tradition not to mark graves, and in fact, there was no strong tomb tradition associated with Mongol culture at this time. It is likely that bodies would have been left for wild animals and birds to dispose of. Most accounts of the burial of Genghis Khan describe how the funeral procession was flanked by many soldiers, and as they progressed to a location near his birthplace, everyone they encountered was killed to preserve the secret of where the body of the khan was to be taken. It is believed that servants, horses, and virgins were buried with him to accompany him to the next life. Some accounts claim that vast amounts of treasure were buried with him as well.

The gravesite was trampled over many times by hundreds of horsemen, compressing the earth to disguise any telling signs of a burial. An alternative version, where the body was laid out and trampled into the earth by horsemen, would have been in keeping with some Mongol customs. Whatever the true nature of the disposal of the body, it seems likely that they did everything possible to hide the location of Genghis' final resting place. Some versions of the story say that trees were planted over the site, but the commonly accepted version is that a river was diverted to flow over the site and hide it forever from potential grave robbers. In one final, fittingly gruesome act, everyone involved in the burial and hiding of the grave was killed. If knowledge of the true location did survive, it has now been lost. Rumors and legends are all that remain of the story.

There are a number of sacred sites associated with Genghis Khan which are treated as places of pilgrimage and spirituality by his descendants. One is a location in Yijinhuoluo ("Holy Land of the Emperor"), which is revered as the place where Genghis stopped his horse, dropped his horsewhip, and became entranced by the lush landscape, chanting the following words:

A place where flowers and deer inhabits,

A home where hoopoes give birth to their babies,

A terra where the declined dynasty revives,

And a garden where a gray-haired man enjoys his life.

The story continues that he told his servants to bury him in this place after he died, and when the funeral procession passed by, the wheels of the cart would not turn, and the servants remembered his request. Some people believe that his ashes were interred at this place, but it is not widely believed by historians that he was actually buried there. However, a mausoleum was built there in his honor, and this became the official sacred place dedicated to Genghis Khan. His descendants created a series of eight sacred white camps where they honored him in Mongolia, and this was later moved to the location of the mausoleum.

The mausoleum itself, which is better known as the Lord's Enclosure, has an interesting story of its own. It was lifted and moved in 1939 by the Chinese in order to protect it from possible damage by the invading Japanese forces. Political instability and numerous wars meant that the mausoleum was moved a number of times, traveling hundreds of miles and spending time in monasteries under the protection of monks before returning to Inner Mongolia, in modern-day northern China. Sadly, in 1968, the mausoleum and the relics within it were damaged by Red Guards during the Cultural Revolution. Attempts were made in the 1970s to restore the relics, and a statue of Genghis Khan was erected at the site.

It remains an important tourist attraction for visitors to Inner Mongolia, and it is an important part of the cultural heritage of the Mongolian people. Offerings are routinely brought to the place, candles and incense are burnt, and prayers are recited.

The Search for Genghis Khan

The secret location of the tomb of Genghis Khan, if in fact such a tomb even exists, is an enduring mystery that is important for those who seek a spiritual connection to Genghis or who treasure the folklore that surrounds his life and death. Historians and archaeologists are also extremely keen to find the lost tomb. Rumors of vast treasures inspire not just the academic experts but also treasure hunters to travel to Mongolia in search of the hidden resting place of the great leader.

If the stories are true, then great stores of wealth worth billions in currency and far more in terms of cultural and artistic heritage could be lying beneath the Mongolian plains. However, Mongolian culture forbids the disturbing of gravesites; graveyards and tombs are considered forbidden places which should be left alone. This makes it extremely difficult for researchers to conduct any investigations into the areas they consider most likely to contain the grave of Genghis Khan.

There have been a number of promising searches that have claimed to come close to finding the burial place; for instance, archaeologists believe they have found the palace of Genghis Khan which is believed to have been near his burial site. A number of promising clues have been uncovered, but the reluctance of the Mongolian people to permit any excavation which may disturb the Great Khan and the difficulty of the terrain means that the secret is still intact. The grave of Genghis Khan is also rumored to be under an ancient curse that states that whoever opens it will suffer and unleash a great war upon the world. There are even stories of terrible accidents and freak events occurring to those who have sought the grave. Despite this, the search for Genghis Khan and his treasures will no doubt continue as his life, death, and legacy continue to both horrify and intrigue.

Chapter 9 – The Mongol Empire After Genghis Khan

At the time of Genghis Khan's death, the Mongol Empire stretched from the Sea of Japan to the Caspian Sea, including the modern countries of Mongolia, Kyrgyzstan, Tajikistan, Uzbekistan, and Turkmenistan in their entirety, nearly all of Kazakhstan, about half of China, and into Russia, Iran, Afghanistan, Pakistan, India, and North Korea. Even at this point, before it had reached the peak of its expansion, it was nearly thrice the size of the Roman Empire at its largest. It was already the largest empire the world had ever seen. The Mongol Empire was regarded with a mixture of awe and fear by nations far and wide. The Mongol army had developed into an experienced war machine, but even in places where the army had not reached, the stories had certainly gone before them. The reputation of the Mongols was fearsome enough to compel many high-ranking people in neighboring territories to defect. Even the death of Genghis Khan himself, when it finally became known, was not enough to calm the fears of the nations he had not lived to defeat.

Genghis Khan's chosen successor, Ögedei, set about fulfilling his father's ambitions. Ögedei was apparently a very charismatic leader with a strong personality and an intelligent mind, much like his father. However, he did not have the same leadership capabilities or military acumen as Genghis had demonstrated, and so, he relied heavily on the advisors he inherited from his father. His brothers, sons, and grandsons, despite their personal grievances and squabbles, were capable and powerful commanders who he could rely on for guidance. Like his father, he awarded responsibility to those who deserved it and who would serve the empire well. This was much to the benefit of the empire and its citizens as Ögedei was rather fond of feasting and merriment, and he had to be watched carefully due to his increasingly dangerous alcohol habit. In later life, this tendency to drink in excess became much more serious. Having promised his advisors to drink fewer cups of alcohol each day, Ögedei simply increased his cup size, and his alcoholism grew to become more of a threat to his reign and his life.

Expansion West and East

The Mongol Empire continued to grow rapidly under the rule of Ögedei. He was aware of his father's hopes for the empire, and he had the support of his father's well-organized generals and commanders to carry out the necessary campaigns. This began with expansions to the west, with victories over the Bashkirs and Bulgars of the western steppe. The final conquest of the Khwarazmian Empire, who had already been subdued under Genghis, was soon completed, and several other smaller Persian states yielded easily to the Mongols. In the east, with victory over Manchuria and the Eastern Xia regime, the Mongol Empire's power was becoming increasingly secure across Central Asia.

Having consolidated the power of the empire and reaffirmed his position as leader, Ögedei initiated what would be the final push in the campaign to defeat the Jin dynasty. The Jin had long been a thorn in the side of the Mongol Empire; the war between the Mongols and the Jurchens of the Jin dynasty had been raging for over twenty years. Ögedei used typical Mongol tactics, leading one army into battle himself while Tolui, his brother, led another. When the armies met at the capital city of Kaifeng, they were commanded by the top general, Subutai. Subutai led the infamous Siege of Kaifeng in 1232, holding the city under siege for almost a year. Despite putting up a tough defense, the city succumbed to starvation and crumbled under the constant barrage of attacks from the Mongols. This was the beginning of the end for the Jin dynasty. While the ruler escaped and petitioned the Song dynasty of south China for aid, they refused, siding with the Mongols, and in early 1234, the Jin dynasty was finally defeated. This was a period when the Mongol army itself was expanding as quickly as the empire was as more and more defectors from Chinese dynasties joined the Mongols. The empire seemed to be unstoppable, and confidence grew among the people and soldiers.

It was now time for the most distant and ambitious campaign the Mongol armies had ever undertaken. Commanding generals moved into what we now call Russia, while others moved farther into Eastern Europe. Russia, Poland, Bulgaria, Serbia, and Hungary all fell to the Mongols. They brought experienced generals, battle-hardened warriors, and something that the Europeans had never seen before—gunpowder. Using siege weaponry such as giant catapults, the Mongols were able to propel bombs into settlements and armies alike. This was an entirely new technology that had originated in East Asia, and it must have been terrifying to the Europeans who had little to no experience of incendiary devices. The conquered lands in Europe became known as the Golden Horde. It formed the northwestern section of the Mongol Empire and functioned as a separate khanate (kingdom ruled by a minor khan) presided over by Batu Khan, the eldest son of Jochi and grandson of Genghis Khan.

The campaign to conquer Russia, or Rus' as it was then known, started in 1235 when Ögedei first commanded his nephew, Batu, to lead the campaign and ended with the final battle for the Russian capital, Kiev, in 1240. It was a particularly merciless campaign, with devastation following in the wake of the vast armies as they moved across the land. Province after province was captured, and few who resisted were spared from the slaughter. Their capital, Kiev, was nearly completely destroyed.

Similar destruction took place across Europe, with hundreds of thousands of people losing their lives and hundreds of towns and cities being razed to the ground. Food stores were destroyed, the land was damaged, and settlements ransacked. This meant that those who were not killed or enslaved by the Mongol armies were condemned to poverty, starvation, and disease. The number of people killed indirectly through the actions of the Mongol armies can only be guessed at.

The advance of the Mongol armies in Europe was halted when word reached Batu Khan of the death of Ödegei, his uncle, in December 1241. Batu raced back to Mongolia, abandoning his campaign in Europe because a far more pressing concern had arisen: who would succeed Ögedei and become the next Great Khan? Had it not been for the death of Ögedei, the plan was to invade first Vienna and then move farther west into the Holy Roman Empire, and many experts believe that the Mongols would have been successful had they continued with this agenda.

Power Struggle

Ögedei's widow, Töregene, claimed leadership of the empire after her husband's death. Despite the fact that she was a woman and there were blood descendants of Genghis and Ögedei who were hungry for the role, she persuaded many of the other Mongol leaders to support her reign. She ruled as regent for five years from 1241 until 1246 before handing over power to her son, Güyük. Batu Khan, son of Jochi, contested this, and there was a bitter rivalry between the two. Fractures in the family no longer had the pacifying influence of Genghis or Ögedei to stop them from spilling over into violence, and so, tensions mounted. Güyük rode out to confront Batu with his soldiers in 1248 but died on the journey before he could reach him. This did not mean that the power passed to Batu, as he might have hoped; instead, it went to their cousin, Möngke. Möngke was another grandson of Genghis Khan, and he ascended to become the Great Khan in 1251. Möngke Khan was seen as a safer option for the Mongol Empire and was felt to be a good compromise. Batu felt able to support Möngke's claim to power more than he could support any other candidate, and there was some reluctant healing of the rifts in the family as the rivalry between Batu and Güyük was allowed to cool down. Batu once again turned his attention back to his planned invasion of Europe, but he, too, died before he could initiate his great campaign into the west of the continent.

The Empire under Möngke Khan

Möngke Khan was a disciplined and traditional leader who oversaw the expansion of the Mongol Empire while implementing some much-needed economic reforms. He was very concerned with overhauling the economic and administrative regimes, and in 1253, he set up a department to deal with installing economic stability through the control of paper money production. He also tried to reduce the number of debts built up by the rather decadent aristocracy. Möngke implemented stricter controls on spending and gift-giving among the ruling families and taxed trade by conducting a census of all people and the property they possessed. He also forbade his generals from looting or demanding goods from citizens. These measures of relative austerity were combined with various techniques designed to promote trade as he attempted to make the Mongol Empire more efficient and profitable. This did not necessarily make him a popular leader; there were multiple riots and revolts against the taxation system. Despite the fact that he did levy the harshest taxes against the wealthiest in society, his changes were resisted fiercely by the lower classes as well. However, he managed to put down any resistance he encountered and hold on to his power.

Khanates

The Mongol Empire had been divided into khanates after the death of Genghis Khan. A khanate was a territory, or kingdom, which was a part of the Mongol Empire but which was presided over by a ruler (a "loyal khan") who was answerable to the Great Khan. The khanates were kept in the family of Genghis Khan, making it a return to an aristocracy of sorts, which Genghis Khan himself had largely eradicated in his homeland of Mongolia. Möngke Khan's control of the khanates was threatened by his unpopular taxation and growing civil unrest among the occupied populations. This was especially true in the areas farther from the capital of the empire. Those with very different cultures and traditions were most likely to resent the Mongol rule, and so, each khanate was ruled according to the culture of the people and the attitude of the ruler, meaning that the khanates became increasingly different and separate.

Rapid Expansion under Möngke Khan

Under Möngke's general's command, the Mongol armies surged into the Middle East. Iraq and Syria, particularly the cities of Aleppo and Damascus, were attacked and conquered with the same merciless brutality that had become the trademark of all of the Mongol military campaigns. Möngke rapidly expanded the empire's territory, and in just a few years, they had reached all the way to the Mediterranean Sea. The human cost was massive. At the same time, to the east, the conquest of China and Vietnam was under way. Möngke himself, along with his brother Kublai, fought against the Chinese in an attempt to finally add all of the Chinese territories to the Mongol Empire. His army was overcome by rapidly spreading disease, which cost him many men. Möngke Khan himself died of illness contracted on a military campaign in China in 1259.

The Mongolian Civil War

The death of Möngke Khan led to what became known as the Toluid Civil War. This was fought between Möngke's two younger brothers, Ariq Böke and Kublai. Both men sought to succeed their brother, and neither would step back and allow a peaceful transfer of power. The tribes were once again at war with one another, and this tension highlighted the danger to the empire if unity among the Mongol people themselves could not be maintained. After a bloody battle, Kublai was the victor when Ariq Böke surrendered in 1264. Kublai, who had already assumed the role of Great Khan in 1260, was now able to rule without interference from his brother.

The Empire under Kublai

In 1279, Kublai's armies managed to defeat the Song dynasty to finally complete the ultimate conquest of China, something that his predecessors had only dreamt of. In 1271, eight years before the complete downfall of the Song dynasty, Kublai Khan created the Yuan dynasty to rule over the Mongol heartlands, China, and, nominally, the whole of the Mongol Empire. Kublai Khan was the very first non-Han Chinese leader to rule over the whole of China.

As such, he claimed the title of Emperor of China and styled himself as a great Chinese emperor in order to win over the remaining resistant Chinese. Kublai put his grandfather Genghis Khan into the imperial records as the acknowledged founder, giving him the posthumous name Taizu, making Genghis the official founder of the Yuan dynasty.

Kublai also moved the capital of the empire from Mongolia to Khanbaliq, also known as Dadu, in China, a city we now know as Beijing. This did not sit well with the traditional Mongols, who felt Kublai was leaving behind the traditional Mongol ways by embracing Chinese culture. However, Kublai was faced with a difficult choice as ruler; a select Mongol aristocracy with little experience of the more highly developed society in China could not rule using the old Mongol ways. In order to hold onto power, the Mongols would have to adapt and embrace some of the Chinese ways. This was best described by one of Kublai's advisors who reportedly said, "I have heard that one can conquer the empire on horseback, but one cannot govern it on horseback." For things to stay the same, i.e., the Mongol Empire to remain, then things would have to change.

Kublai was a very different type of leader than the Chinese rulers who had gone before. He was interested in developing Chinese culture and improving the way of life. Although Kublai Khan favored Buddhism, he was relatively religiously tolerant. However, like his Mongol ancestors he forbade the Jewish (*shechita*) or Muslim (*dhabihah*) legal codes. Furthermore, circumcision was also strictly forbidden. On the other hand, he made far-reaching infrastructure changes. By developing the road and water travel systems and setting up postal stations, he opened China up and made trade and travel easier. China became a great empire under Kublai, with a thriving arts community, generous investments in science, and the founding of thousands of public schools. A new social structure emerged, with the Mongols at the top, untaxed and supported by the lower-class Chinese.

War continued at the edges of the empire as Kublai continued to push the boundaries of his territory in southeast Asia. Many failed attempts to annex Japan proved to be a costly burden on the Mongol Empire. Tensions remained high, and there was increasing conflict between the traditional Mongol way of life, represented by the government and the military, and the new Chinese dynasty. Kublai struggled to achieve stability and tried to pacify the Mongols by continuing the expansion of the empire beyond what was economically viable. With a constant pull in many different directions and the trauma of the deaths of his empress and his heir, it seems the Great Khan buckled under the pressure, succumbing to an excess of food and alcohol. He died in 1294, and despite his difficult period of rule, he remains highly regarded for the rich and diverse cultural renaissance that took place in China under his rule. The Yuan dynasty continued under various leaders until 1368.

The Growth of the Khanates

After the death of Kublai Khan, there was growing unrest among the Mongols. There had been a number of minor civil wars between various factions, and the khanates were more disparate than ever. The Mongol Empire was divided up into four main sections: The Khanate of the Great Khan (also known as the Yuan dynasty of China), the Golden Horde, the Ilkhanate, and the Chagatai Khanate.

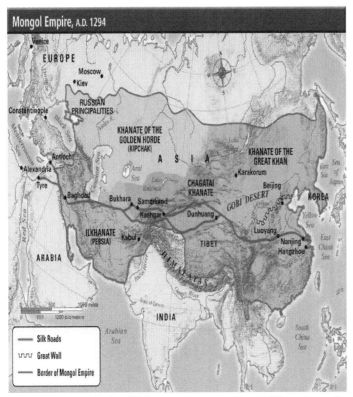

Mongol Empire, A.D. 1294

Silk Roads
Great Wall
Border of Mongol Empire

The Yuan and the Ilkhanate were close allies, but the Ilkhanate had its own troubles with uprisings among various Islamic groups. In 1304, a peace treaty was signed that secured peaceful relations between the khanates who agreed upon their allegiance to the Yuan dynasty. While this reduced tension, each khanate continued to function as a separate entity, developing in directions that soon evolved to be so different that clashes and competition for power were inevitable.

For the meantime, within the Mongol Empire itself, there was a period of relative peace and prosperity. For the first time in history, there was a single government ruling over regions from East Asia to West Asia and East Europe, and a huge cultural and economic exchange took place that changed the world forever. The effects of this period of human history are still being felt today as an intrinsic part of our shared history. This period was known as the Pax Mongolica.

Chapter 10 – Pax Mongolica

While the Pax Mongolica, meaning Mongol Peace, may sound like an end to the violence of the past while a new era of peaceful existence dominated, that wasn't quite the case. The Mongol armies continued to work hard to expand the Mongol Empire in many bloody military campaigns, but life within the empire itself was relatively settled. The strict Yassa code meant that misdemeanors were severely punished, and so, crime fell. People were relatively secure and able to build up their own households and improve their situations. The Mongol soldiers were able to accrue wealth instead of having to hand over looted goods to the aristocracy, and so, the wealth and quality of life of the general population increased. New innovations, often a result of great minds who had been spared by the Mongol armies for the skills they could offer, also made life easier. The borders of the empire had been pushed back so far that there was nothing to fear from foreign invaders for those at the heart of the empire. The unified empire was much more stable and secure, and this allowed communication and travel to thrive, resulting in the spread of both goods and ideas.

Trade and Prosperity

Genghis Khan himself had been keen to promote trade and facilitate economic growth. The whole time he was masterminding great military advances he was also incubating a thriving trade system.

Trade was an essential part of life in the Mongol Empire; the Mongolian steppe itself did not provide enough food or other goods to serve the people, and the Mongol tribes became increasingly interested in goods sourced from farther afield that could make their lives easier. Prior to the Mongol Empire being established, trade flourished only between allies, so economic growth was very dependent on political stability. As the Mongol Empire absorbed the many different territories into one unified regime, there were no political barriers to trade, allowing it to flourish.

Merchants traveling through the Mongol Empire could rely upon protection from attacks. In fact, they were often used to carry out other missions for the Mongols, serving as diplomats and carriers of information. Trade routes were increasingly used, and the more well-traveled they became, the better maintained they were and the easier it was for traveling merchants to access supplies and shelter as they traveled, enabling them to go farther and trade more. Each conquest by the Mongols added to the trade routes, gave the empire access to more skilled people, and brought an influx of new and innovative goods. By the time of the Pax Mongolica, when life was a lot more settled and prosperous across the empire, trade routes were well developed. The main route that stretched from the Mediterranean all the way to China is known as the Silk Road.

The Mongol Empire and the Silk Road

While parts of what we call the Silk Road had been in existence since as far back as the 3rd century BCE, much of it had been abandoned over time, as shifting political regimes and the threat of attacks and pillaging had made it no longer a viable option for merchants. Genghis Khan saw the potential in the old route and exerted his control over the roads as a priority. His aim was to encourage trade that was in the interest of the empire; trade could be taxed and controlled, and the routes could prove useful to his spies and messengers. Genghis got rid of any existing trading posts along the route and replaced them with his own. The Mongols set up trading posts, built bridges, shored up roads, and established traditional Persian inns known as *caravanserais* to provide shelter and supplies. They even planted tall trees alongside the roads to cut out the glare of the sun and provide shade for travelers. This era of the trade route's history, when the Silk Road was under the control of the Mongols, became known as the fourth Silk Road.

There was also a sea route which functioned in much the same way as the Silk Road did on land. This was a period of rapid development of maritime technology, especially as the Mongol Empire brought together some of the brightest and most innovative engineering minds from across many different subjugated territories. Sea routes began as a minor part of the trade economy of the empire, with minor routes around the Chinese landmass, and in time, they became more and more expansive with expeditions all the way to India, Arabia, and even Africa.

While the land route was called the Silk Road, there was a lot more than silk making its way from East to West and vice versa during the Mongol reign. Previous periods of the Silk Road's use had seen the routes used for trade in a variety of commodities; however, it became most famous for its trade in silk, a very precious commodity that emerged from China and was in high demand in the West. In the new era of the Silk Road, precious metals, gems, and pearls were transported, along with crafted goods such as ceramics and carpets. Medicine made its way from China into the West, and expensive spices from all regions were widely exported. From Europe came linen, cloth, fine metals, and horses.

The thriving trade along the Silk Road led to the rapid expansion of towns and cities along the route. Garrisons were placed at strategic points to protect travelers and traders, and few were prepared to risk the wrath of the Mongol armies by thieving or looting. It was famously said that a maiden could travel the length of the Mongol Empire along the routes laden with gold and nobody would harm her. There was also a huge move away from corrupt taxes and cheating the system to a new, more open approach that aimed for fairness. There was a new standardized system of measures and weights that made trade less liable to corruption, and the strict rules established by the Yassa code meant that it was forbidden to steal from traders or molest them in any way.

The Flow of Ideas

It wasn't just tangible goods that you could hold in your hands that made the long journey from one side of the Mongol Empire to the other and beyond. Ideas and innovations also spread across the empire and reached Europe. Some of the fundamental ideas that we still value in our own society made their way to the West through the Silk Road and other trade routes that emerged during the period of the Pax Mongolica.

The Muslim world exported advances in science, astronomy, and mathematics that carried new ideas and concepts to both the Europeans and the peoples of East Asia. Manufacturing techniques, such as fabric production, paper-making, and printing methods, were shared. New ideas about money had a seismic impact on European society; paper money that made it easier to travel with large sums (coins were far too heavy for large transactions), credit that made it possible to conduct business on a larger scale, and deposit banking that kept wealth secure all came from the East. In fact, the concept of insurance is thought to have emerged from Eastern lands, spreading across the Silk Road and into Europe.

New foods and culinary ideas also reached Europe. Spices became easier to get a hold of, and cinnamon, nutmeg, ginger, and pepper were new and exciting flavors to try. Travelers and merchants brought with them not just the wares they were selling but also a sense of their own culture, and this must have been extremely intriguing for the people of the time. For the majority of people, this was the first time they had experienced other cultures which were very different from their own.

Ideas on spirituality and religion had a huge impact as they, too, moved across the continent. Not only did merchants and explorers bring with them their own religious beliefs, but missionaries were also able to travel along the trade routes and share their belief systems with others. The Mongol Empire was famously tolerant of all religions, and the countries it had absorbed had citizens of many different faiths. As these peoples spread out across the empire, and in many cases intermarried, religious ideas were shared more freely than at any other time. Cities often had many different places of worship dedicated to different religious traditions, and with religious leaders exempt from taxation, diversity was actively encouraged. Many of these religious beliefs became blended as ideas were exchanged.

Arts and Crafts

Genghis Khan had encouraged the production of crafts for trade, and his successors also continued to promote arts and crafts. The Mongol people themselves were not major producers of art; a nomadic lifestyle in a difficult climate with the frequent threat from enemies is not exactly conducive to the production of fine art! However, the Mongols did appreciate the arts and became indulgent patrons of the arts in the empire. During the period of the Pax Mongolica, there was a huge cultural revolution, with a surge of artistic creativity and a flourishing of new decorative and fine arts.

Many skilled artisans from across the empire were taken to Mongolia itself in order to transform the capital city of Karakorum. They designed buildings, decorated the city, and created a thriving artistic community. Almost every aspect of the arts flourished under the Pax Mongolica, from ceramics to decorative metalworking and from theatrical productions to musical innovations.

Just as ideas spread across the empire, imagery, too, found its way from one side of the empire to the other. Chinese art flourished under the Yuan dynasty, and Chinese iconography began to appear in European art, while in Persia, the miniature illustrated histories developed. Under the patronage of the Mongol aristocracy, a golden age of arts and crafts was established that many people regard as the foundation for various artistic practices still in use today.

In musical terms, the Mongols had always been lovers of music, especially singing. *Höömij*, or throat singing, is the musical practice most associated with the Mongolian people. Associated with the spiritual belief in animism, that all things contain a spirit, *höömij* seeks to replicate the sounds of nature using multiple pitches produced by the throat and voice, giving the impression of a number of voices singing at once. This may have originated among the herdsmen on the vast grasslands where sound would travel a long way, and it came to have special cultural significance, especially in a time of great cultural exchange.

Explorers

It wasn't just goods and ideas that traveled throughout the Mongol Empire; there was also a host of adventurers and explorers who was keen to see the new world. While few traders ever traveled the whole of the Silk Road, instead trading at trading centers where goods would be exchanged and then moved on again (in much the same way that messages passed through the empire using a relay system), there were some people who traveled the road in order to experience it and explore the lands that lay beyond their own.

Marco Polo

The most famous of all explorers to explore the Mongol Empire has got to be Marco Polo. Born in Venice, he first began his epic series of journeys across Europe and Asia when he was seventeen years old. His father and uncle had already traveled in the Mongol Empire and had returned to Venice after sixteen years of traveling to find that Marco had been born and that his mother had later died. Marco joined them on their travels as they returned to the court of Kublai Khan, bringing holy oil from Jerusalem and documents from the pope. After a journey that took almost four years, they arrived, and Marco met Kublai Khan sometime between 1271 and 1275. His father offered the services of his son to the khan. Marco appears to have developed a favored relationship with Kublai Khan, receiving education in his court and becoming a highly prized diplomat. He traveled across China in the service of the Great Khan for the next seventeen years. He mastered many languages, including Mongolian and Chinese, and embraced many Mongol customs. He was very impressed with a lot of what he saw in the Mongol Empire, stating, "of all of men in the world, [the Mongols are] best able to endure exertion and hardship…least costly to maintain and therefore the best adapted for conquering territory and overthrowing kingdoms."

The Polo family wanted to return to Venice, and Kublai Khan reluctantly permitted them to return to their homeland if they agreed to transport a Mongol princess. They agreed, and after a long and dangerous journey, they arrived back in Venice in 1295, much to the surprise of their relatives. They returned in Mongol clothing, bearing diamonds and other precious stones. Unfortunately, they returned in the midst of a war between Venice and Genoa (both independent city-states at this time), and Marco Polo soon found himself on the losing side and ended up in prison.

During his time in prison, Marco met a writer called Rustichello da Pisa, who wrote down Marco's stories of his travels. This written account, *The Travels of Marco Polo* by Rustichello and Polo, became the main source of information for the Western world on China and the Mongol Empire. Translated into many languages, it captured the imagination of the world and secured Marco Polo's legacy as one of the world's most famous explorers. On his release from prison, Marco Polo settled down to married life and business, dying in 1324. The accounts of Yuan dynasty China and the wider Mongol Empire by Marco Polo form some of the few firsthand accounts that historians have on the empire. Over a century later, Christopher Columbus would set sail with his annotated copy of Polo's account in the hope that the knowledge it contained would prove useful when he reached the court of the descendant of Kublai Khan. He had no way of knowing that by 1492, when he was embarking on his epic journey, the Mongol Empire would have already disintegrated.

Rabban Bar Ṣawma

Rabban Bar Ṣawma was a Turkic Chinese traveler and envoy of the Mongol Empire who made the journey across a large part of the Mongol Empire from east to west, as opposed to Marco Polo's west to east. Born in Zhongdu (modern Beijing), Bar Ṣawma became a Nestorian Christian monk in his early twenties and headed west on a pilgrimage to Jerusalem. He reached the Ilkhanate but could not travel farther than Baghdad because of fighting and civil unrest, and so, he did not reach Jerusalem. Instead, he spent time in various

Nestorian monasteries before being summoned as an envoy to the Mongol khan of the Ilkhanate, Abaqa. An intelligent and capable man, Rabban Bar Ṣawma became an important diplomatic figure as well as an important teacher and authority figure in the Nestorian church.

Bar Ṣawma was later sent by Abaqa's son as an envoy from the Mongols to Europe, where he was received by various European monarchs as well as Pope Nicholas IV in Rome in 1288. He stayed with King Philip IV of France and also had a meeting with English King Edward I. His time in Europe was part of a wider attempt to join the Europeans with the Mongols in a European-Mongol alliance, which was never fully realized as neither Philip IV nor Edward I would agree to such an alliance.

Well educated and perceptive, Bar Ṣawma kept a detailed diary of his travels. While the stories of Marco Polo give a view of the East from the perspective of a Westerner, the diary of Bar Ṣawma gives the opposite: a view of the West from an Eastern native. The juxtaposition of these two texts gives great insight into the Mongol Empire and into medieval life, politics, and change across Asia and Europe.

The End of the Pax Mongolica

Throughout the period known as the Pax Mongolica, tensions between rival factions bubbled under the surface, sometimes erupting into squabbling and even violence. The khanates were more separate and disconnected than ever, and the death of Kublai Khan in 1294 was the catalyst for the further breakdown of relations between the leaders of the khanates. Kublai was succeeded by his son Temür, but the power of the Great Khan had been seriously eroded by this point. The Mongol Empire had essentially been divided into four separate states: The Yuan dynasty, the Golden Horde, the Chagatai Khanate, and the Ilkhanate. The united Mongol Empire was no longer united. Expansion had slowed, and they were beginning to find themselves on the losing side of battles. Not only that, but the economic situation was perilous, and rivalry between the khanates mounted.

Chapter 11 – The End of an Empire

With the khanates developing in different directions and old rivalries meeting new grievances and causing flare-ups of tension between the khanate leaders, the days of the Pax Mongolica came to an end in the mid-14th century. The divided empire was weaker, as many of the minor khans who ruled the khanates were incompetent and their rule disorganized. However, there was an increasing desire to be separate from the Mongol Empire, to have independence and freedom to make their own rules—especially when the Great Khan was so immersed in Chinese culture.

Each time a leader died (oftentimes under suspicious circumstances), chaos would reign. There had never been an established way to hand over power from one leader to the next in a peaceful manner. With no protocol that could be agreed upon and followed, leadership bids were fraught with violent opposition and disorder. This infighting and rivalry led to the breakdown of the khanates, a further dilution of power that was essentially the main cause of the decline of the Mongol Empire.

The Breakdown of the Khanates

In the Golden Horde khanate, religious tensions had grown as the khanate adopted Islam as the main religion. In 1359, the leader of the Golden Horde was assassinated by his brother, and in the subsequent struggle to find a new leader and the violent rivalry of the potential candidates who had a claim to power, the khanate began to decline. There was a long period of political and social instability. The Golden Horde had largely lost contact with the Yuan dynasty and the homeland of Mongolia. Even when relative peace resumed, the damage had already been done, and in 1396, the Golden Horde became fractured and broke up into a group of smaller khanates, diluting its power and leaving the Horde vulnerable to attack. Over time, these smaller states were conquered by other forces. While the Crimean Khanate lasted until 1783 and the Kazakh Khanate lasted until 1847, they had long since lost sight of their Mongol origins; besides that, by that point, the Mongol Empire was long gone.

In the Ilkhanate, historically the most loyal of khanates to the Yuan dynasty, religious tension also affected the political and social atmosphere. Slow to convert to Islam, the leaders found themselves with a disgruntled Muslim population. When they did convert to Islam, the leader replaced many Mongol traditions with those of the Muslim population, and in doing so, they lost the support of the Mongol army. In the early 1300s, the Black Death ravaged the Ilkhanate, and the khan of the Ilkhanate and his sons were killed by the plague. Wars and famines decimated the population and left the khanate vulnerable. Splitting into rival states, the Ilkhanate dissolved in 1335.

In the Chagatai Khanate, invasions wore away at their territory. The rebellion of the tribes within the khanate created political instability, and it was split into two in the 1340s. The western section was Muslim and the eastern mainly Buddhist. Each section attempted to legitimize their rule by placing rulers of strong Mongol heritage on the throne, forging a connection back to Genghis Khan that was in name only; these puppet rulers had little power. In time, both sections became fractured and broke up.

In the Yuan Dynasty, the successors of Kublai Khan had very little power over Mongol territory in the other khanates. They were viewed as being Chinese rather than Mongol by the other Mongols. Yet within China, issues of Chinese identity were still a cause of bitterness among the citizens. A fundamental lack of understanding of the Chinese people was a big part of the problem. The Chinese peasantry were mostly farmers. Mongol leaders, however, had never made agriculture a priority. It was not a part of Mongol culture and not well understood by successive leaders. As a result, policies which made life difficult for agricultural workers, such as permitting crops to be ravaged by hunting expeditions and forbidding farmers from protecting their crops from animals, led to huge resentment. Something as seemingly arbitrary as the Mongol preference for hunting and rearing livestock over planting and harvesting crops led to a fundamental rift between those in power and their subjects. Dissent in China often began with the lower classes, so these grudges were dangerous.

The incompetence in the aristocracy, as they focused on petty rivalries and led decadent lifestyles, only led to further bitterness and resentment. The people were taxed heavily, especially in the south, which was wealthier. Civil unrest and pillaging by outlaws went unchecked by the armies, and natural disasters such as floods and famines went without aid. The armies had been allowed to decline and were no longer the same ravenous battle-ready troops that had made the Mongol Empire what it was. Instead, numbers declined, and management grew poor. Mongolia had been allowed to decline during this time as well, and so, there were fewer numbers of fresh soldiers coming up through the ranks.

All of these factors allowed pockets of discontent to merge into widespread violent dissent. There were many independent rebellions which sought to weaken Mongol power. These rebellions were largely led by oppressed people who initially felt deep resentment over the unfair class system rather than actual hatred of the Mongols, but xenophobia was increasing and spreading. A serious financial collapse was almost inevitable as the paper money that the Mongol government relied upon became worthless.

A major rebellion by those still loyal to the old Song dynasty began in 1351, further weakening the Yuan dynasty's power and influence. This was known as the Red Turban Rebellion, and one of the commanders was Zhu Yuanzhang. Soon, the Ming dynasty, founded by Zhu Yuanzhang, sent armies up from the south. While they initially failed to conquer Khanbaliq, the khan, Toghon Temür, had long since fled, and it was only a matter of time before the Ming dynasty defeated any resistance that sprang up. China was conquered by the Ming dynasty in 1368.

Fleeing to Mongolia, the name of Yuan continued, and the Northern Yuan dynasty was established. The Mongols did attempt to regain some of their power over the next few centuries, with occasional forays into China to regain lost territory and reestablish power. None of these attempts were very successful, and of course, rivalries between tribes again only served to weaken them. However, they were able to defend Mongolia from attempts by the Ming dynasty to occupy their country.

Bubonic Plague

While most of the factors that resulted in the end of the Pax Mongolica and the decline of the Mongol Empire can be described as internal issues, there was one major external factor that played a huge role in the decline of the empire and its population. The Great Plague, also known as the Black Death, had a devastating effect on the population of Asia and Europe in the 1300s.

Historians believe that the plague may have originated in Central Asia in rodent populations and was then taken into the west by Mongol soldiers. Fleas infected with the plague could easily travel on the horses and camels, and the Pax Mongolica meant that people and animals were moving faster and farther than ever before along the trade routes, extending the reach of the disease in every direction. The Mongol battle tactic of catapulting corpses into settlements under attack is likely to have added to the spread of plague; plague-ridden bodies infected healthy people in the settlements, and disease spread rapidly under siege conditions.

Trade routes became riddled with the disease, which led to economic decline, but it was the impact on the population that was the worst. Half of the Chinese people were killed by bubonic plague at this time, while at least a quarter and up to half of the European population died.

The Legacy of the Mongol Empire

Through a combination of internal struggles and external hardships, the great Mongol Empire, which had been the largest contiguous land-based empire that the world had ever seen, had first cracked, then fractured, and finally dissolved. However, having united a large part of Asia and Europe as one empire, the Mongol influence was less easily wiped out. The lasting legacy of the Mongol Empire is almost as intriguing as the empire itself.

While many of the states and countries that were absorbed into the Mongol Empire, and those which formed afterward, are unfamiliar to modern onlookers, the empire did shape Asia and Europe into what we see today. China and Russia were forged as unified countries by the advance of the Mongol Empire. In fact, Chinese history and Mongol history are inseparable. The Yuan dynasty period is an essential part of the Chinese cultural heritage, and it continues to exert its influence even today.

Religious history is one of the most profoundly affected aspects of world culture that was shaped by the Mongols. Despite the fact that the Mongols did not persecute any religious group, instead choosing to promote religious tolerance, the empire was indirectly responsible for the spread of Islam across the Middle East. As the western khanates converted to the religion practiced by the majority of their subjects, Islam became the dominant religion far beyond the original boundaries of the khanates. Minor religions that may otherwise have been suppressed or eradicated were afforded protection by the Mongol Empire and were allowed to flourish. It is impossible to track the precise implication that this had on world religion or what the religious makeup of the area might have been had it not been for the religiously tolerant Mongol rulers.

Prosperity had flourished during the period of the Pax Mongolica. While there was a downturn during the instability and unrest of subsequent takeovers of the various parts of the empire, and while plague ravaged the population, the skills, knowledge, and techniques that had been shared freely throughout the empire continued to be used and developed. By sparing those who had something to offer the empire, the Mongols had—brutally, of course—concentrated the talent of the population and spread knowledge across the lands. Technological advancements made during Mongol rule accelerated development across Asia and Europe, with unforetold benefits to the societies that would develop long after the Mongol Empire had declined.

Communication between the East and the West had been opened, and despite political instability, natural disasters, and civil unrest, this communication was never again lost. Explorers such as Marco Polo and Bar Ṣawma had opened the eyes of the world to the wonders of other civilizations. Trade links had given people access to goods that they desired, and this did not simply go away with the end of the Mongol Empire; new trade links were found and connections made because now people had a hunger for the goods and knowledge that other places and other people could offer. In this sense, the Mongol Empire was a major leap toward globalization. Never before had the East and the West been so close and never again would they be entirely separated.

There is no escaping the ultimate legacy of Genghis Khan and the Mongol Empire, and that includes the alteration to the human population on earth. Some experts estimate that around forty million people lost their lives to the Mongol armies. Terrible atrocities were carried out in the name of the empire, and widescale terror ensued. It was a dark time for many of the people of Asia and Europe. Enough people were killed that it is believed there was a cooling effect on the earth—a reversal of global warming. As the horror of two World Wars is still within living memory, we can only begin to imagine the widespread destruction and massacres that had taken place after the Mongols had their way.

Genghis Khan, as the founder of the Mongol Empire, is revered and reviled in turn. His legacy is hotly debated. He was undoubtedly a genocidal dictator who was responsible for possibly around forty million people losing their lives. And yet, many cultures look back on the Mongol Empire as the foundation for their cultural heritage.

The Cult of Genghis Khan

While we do not know exactly what Genghis Khan looked like as he forbade the production of his likeness during his lifetime, most of us have an image in our mind's eye of him. However, descriptions of him often talk of a large red beard and pale skin—not at all what most of us imagine. The "Genghis Khan" in the popular imagination is very different from the reality.

In Mongolia, he features on banknotes and postage stamps, and his portrait is frequently seen in marketing campaigns. The main airport in Mongolia is even called Chinggis Khaan International Airport. Great stories of his life are still told, and he is held in reverence and respect in the schoolroom and beyond. Shrines in his honor have been a part of Mongolian life since the empire held power, and attempts to suppress this worship of him have never succeeded. Even the Han Chinese pay homage to Genghis Khan as the official founder of the Yuan dynasty.

Even in the West, where awe at the success of Genghis Khan is mixed with horror at the means by which he achieved his ends, there is a fascination with the leader. Many films have been made about his life, fictional accounts have been written, and research is ongoing as historians glean what they can about the man. Music, theater, and even video games have all explored the life of Genghis Khan. His mausoleum, shrines, and museums attract hundreds of thousands of tourists every year. However far from the truth our stories of Genghis Khan may be, we can be sure that his life will continue to intrigue and create debates for centuries to come.

Conclusion

When a historical figure leaves a legacy of death and destruction—and no other historical figure did that quite as ferociously as Genghis Khan—the positive impacts that they may have had are often lost. This is how we end up with a history full of caricatures: fictional representations of people who are all good or all bad. It's easier to think of "good guys and bad guys and" "heroes and villains" than to come to grip with a reality that is often extremely uncomfortable. So many of our heroes are only heroes because of our perspective, because we have been raised and taught to view them in a certain way. The reality is that many of the historical figures we revere were capable of immensely cruel and barbaric acts, just as many of those that we are conditioned to revile were capable of noble acts and had some positive impacts.

It seems somehow immoral to point out the good points of a historical villain because it feels like we are trying to redeem him somehow. Genghis Khan is a good example of this; we tend to think of him as a cruel dictator and barbaric murderer, so we are surprised to learn about his more liberal policies, his religious tolerance, or his innovative thinking. Historians have to try to let go of value judgments and try not to view things as good or bad, but in our everyday lives, it is much more difficult not to view the past from a more human viewpoint.

By looking at the historical context of Genghis' life, his childhood and formative years, we can gain real insight into what motivated him and why he chose to make the decisions and form the structures that he did. By examining how his empire was built and how life was for those who lived under its rule, we get a glimpse into a world that we can hardly imagine as it is so different to our own. And yet, the conflicts, the pressures, and the external factors that caused the ultimate decline of the empire are recognizable. We all understand political infighting, family rivalries, competition between siblings, economic instability, and natural disasters.

Finally, by taking a look at how the Mongol Empire shaped the world that was to come, we are able to gain some perspective on the events of the past; we can see how the modern world is built on the foundations of the past, both good and bad.

Here are two other books by Captivating History that we think you would find interesting

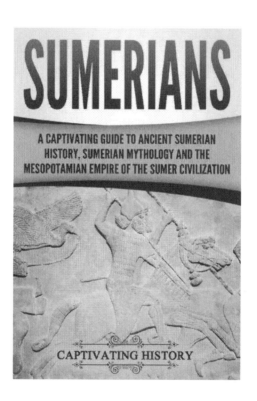

SUMERIANS

A CAPTIVATING GUIDE TO ANCIENT SUMERIAN HISTORY, SUMERIAN MYTHOLOGY AND THE MESOPOTAMIAN EMPIRE OF THE SUMER CIVILIZATION

CAPTIVATING HISTORY

References

Aigle, D. (2015). *The Mongol Empire between Myth and Reality*. Leiden: Brill.

Biography.com. (2019). [online] Available at: https://www.biography.com/dictator/genghis-khan [Accessed 23 Sep. 2019].

Blackstone, W. and Cooley, T. (2003). *Commentaries on the Laws of England*. Clark, N.J.: Lawbook Exchange.

Cartwright, M. and Cartwright, M. (2019). *Genghis Khan*. [online] Ancient History Encyclopedia. Available at: https://www.ancient.eu/Genghis_Khan/ [Accessed 23 Sep. 2019].

Earthy, E. (1955). The Religion of Genghis Khan (A.D. 1162-1227). *Numen*, 2(3), p.228.

En.wikipedia.org. (2019). *Genghis Khan*. [online] Available at: https://en.wikipedia.org/wiki/Genghis_Khan [Accessed 23 Sep. 2019].

Encyclopedia Britannica. (2019). *Genghis Khan | Biography, Conquests, & Facts*. [online] Available at: https://www.britannica.com/biography/Genghis-Khan [Accessed 23 Sep. 2019].

Fitzhugh, W., Rossabi, M. and Honeychurch, W. (2013). *Genghis Khan and the Mongol empire*. [Washington, D.C.]: Arctic Studies

Center, Smithsonian Institution in collaboration with Odyssey Books & Maps.

Hildinger, Erik (1997). *Warriors of The Steppe: Military History of Central Asia, 500 BC To 1700 AD*. Cambridge: De Capo Press.

Jarus, O. (2019). *Genghis Khan, Founder of Mongol Empire: Facts & Biography*. [online] livescience.com. Available at: https://www.livescience.com/43260-genghis-khan.html [Accessed 23 Sep. 2019].

Mclynn, F. (2016). *Genghis Khan - The Man Who Conquered the World*. London: Vintage.

Ratchnevsky, Paul (1991). *Genghis Khan: His Life and Legacy [Čingis-Khan: sein Leben und Wirken]*. tr. & ed. Thomas Nivison Haining. Oxford, UK; Cambridge, Massachusetts, US: B. Blackwell.

Scott, K. (1973). The Successors of Genghis Khan, by Rashid al-Din TabibThe Successors of Genghis Khan, by Rashid al-Din Tabib. Translated by J. A. Boyle. Columbia University Press, New York, 1971. In Canada: McGill-Queen's University Press. 346 pp. *Canadian Journal of History*, 8(1), pp.83-84.

Weatherford, J. (2005). *Genghis Khan and the Making of the Modern World*. Enskede: TPB.

Where Did the Mongol Empire Come from Medieval? Mongol Ideas of People, State and Empire. (2011). *Inner Asia*, 13(2), pp.211-237.

Printed in Poland
by Amazon Fulfillment
Poland Sp. z o.o., Wrocław

53179452R00061